TRAVEL BY
COLOUR

A VISUAL GUIDE TO THE WORLD

CONTENTS

PINK
90

KALEIDOSCOPE
106

GOLD
120

SILVER
132

WHITE
140

GREY
158

INTRODUCTION

The yellow town of Izamal in Mexico. The pink city of Jaipur. And the famous blue hole of Belize. The world is full of colourful places. And if you're somebody who really likes a particular hue, this is the book for you. We have curated a collection of photographs of 400 places and phenomena, from great migrations of orange monarch butterflies and the sweeping spring blooms of wildflowers and blossoms to magnificent design, architecture and festivals. The images are organised across 12 chapters, each dedicated to a single colour.

We know how our mood can change when we're immersed in a colour and a setting: the soothing greens of a forest (here, the swaying fronds of Kamakura bamboo forest in Japan), the calming blue seas of Capri and Sicily, the energising red flashes of a dragon dance in China's new year festivities or a flock of rowdy scarlet macaws as they fly through the Peruvian rainforest.

Colour is also a signal, sometimes an invitation, sometimes a warning. The gold-covered temples of Asia signified holy power and wealth, intended to inspire awe. The beautiful poison dart frogs of Central and South America (see p74) are also very deadly.

And sometimes the absence of colour is just as entrancing. Witness the dances of the red-crowned cranes of Hokkaido against the snow, as they reaffirm their pairings. Or for an even emptier canvas for your imagination, visit the pale dunes of America's newest national park, White Sands in New Mexico.

It's also possible to tell the time by colour. A wave of pink cherry blossom breaks over Japan in spring. In fall, leaves in New England turn a thousand different shades of orange and pumpkins line the roadsides of Illinois. And if there are red fruits flying through the air, it must be Valencia's La Tomatina festival in August.

We hope this books inspires you to explore this colourful planet.

RED

© MATT MUNRO / LONELY PLANET

© YULENOCHEKK / GETTY IMAGES

© PBBOZAC 2017 / SHRUB

BOLOGNA, Italy

You'd be forgiven for thinking one of Bologna's nicknames, *la rossa*, references its many medieval red rooftops. In fact, it principally alludes to the city's long-held left leanings, having been a free commune, a hub for workers' rights, Italy's anti-fascist and Resistance capital during WWII, and a stronghold of Communist support for centuries.

MILAN, Italy

Northern Italy is home to some of the world's most stylish cars. At the Alfa Romeo museum in Arese, near Milan, you'll find the sleek 1950s 1900 C52 Disco Volante (pictured). Ferrari's take on classic red can be seen at Turin's Museo Nazionale dell'Automobile, where almost 200 cars are beautifully displayed in a three-floor 1960s building.

MOSCOW, Russia

On an autumn morning the sun lights up St Basil's Cathedral on Red Square, the most recognisable church in Russia, if not the world. Built in the 16th century by order of Ivan the Terrible, its construction took just six years, and may have been speeded up by the use of a new material, brick, over a timber frame.

DAIGOJI TEMPLE, Japan *(previous page)*

Autumn foliage from lakeside maple and gingko trees surrounds the Bentendo Hall, one of the most picturesque parts of the Daigoji temple complex. This Shingon Buddhist temple in Fushimi-ku, near Kyoto, is particularly beautiful around late November, when the autumn colours, reflected in the lake, are at their most striking.

GALÁPAGOS NATIONAL PARK, Ecuador
During the breeding season, the male great frigatebird on Genovesa Island hugely inflates its gular sac in a bid to attract passing females. With a wingspan of 205–230cm (81–91in), it's not quite as large as the other Galápagos species of frigatebird; the aptly named magnificent frigatebird boasts a 217–244cm (85–96in) wingspan, and shares its relative's impressive inflation abilities.

CÉRET, France
The 25,000 cherry trees in the Pyrénées-Orientales orchards of Céret begin to produce the first of France's huge cherry output as early as March, but playing it safe, the annual cherry festival is held in May. Expect cherry beer, cherry wine, cherry pie, cherry burgers, cherries on toast. . . and of course thousands of cherries.

BEIJING, China
Dragon dancers perform at a park in Beijing on the fourth day of the Lunar New Year festivities. Part of the Spring Festival Holiday, the start of a new year in China is the most important festival of the year, marked with night upon night of firework displays, temple fairs and numerous displays of dance and music.

SAN FRANCISCO, USA *(facing page)*
Fog envelops the Golden Gate bridge almost 70% of the year — making it a tough job keeping it painted in its bespoke 'international orange'. The colour was championed by consulting architect Irving Morrow, who felt its reddish hue would perfectly complement the grey of the fog, the green of the hills, and the blue of water and sky.

FLANDERS, Belgium
'In Flanders fields the poppies grow: between the crosses, row on row. . .' Probably the most celebrated of the WWI poems, these lines were penned by Canadian John McCrae in homage to a lost friend. As war ravaged the countryside its conditions stimulated the growth of poppies, which still bloom on the Western Front battlefields through late spring and early summer.

LONDON, England
The Tower of London Yeomen Warders, more commonly known as Beefeaters, only don this red and gilt formal dress when they're attending state occasions, or when the monarch visits the Tower. Originally designed in 1549, the uniform, and its day-to-day counterpart, the blue and red 'undress uniform' introduced in 1858, are made-to-measure for each Yeoman.

EASTERN STATES, USA
You can catch the vibrant northern cardinal in woodlands, gardens, shrubland and wetlands across large swathes of the eastern USA, where it's the official bird of seven states (Illinois, Indiana, Kentucky, North Carolina, Ohio, Virginia and West Virginia) — more than any other species. The brilliant crimson-red colour is only present in the male.

LONDON, England

The classic old-style Routemaster London bus, complete with a conductor or 'clippie', is part of a dying breed, with just ten in service on route number 15, running the popular tourist route between Tower Hill and Trafalgar Square on spring and summer weekends. But queues of their modern counterparts can always be seen snaking along Regent Street and Oxford Street, or circling Piccadilly Circus like so many 21st-century wagons.

MOUNT RAINIER, USA

This blood moon, shot from Washington state's Mount Rainier, is a rare phenomenon that never fails to impress, wherever and whenever it appears. Not that that's very often...a totally eclipsed blood moon should be visible in May 16 2022, after which you'll have to wait until March 14 2025 to enjoy the spectacle.

SARAWAK, Malaysia

The largest flower in the world (growing to more than a metre in diameter) and probably the smelliest, the fleshy rafflesia wouldn't win any best in bloom prizes, and in any case would be hard to judge given its inaccessible habitats, rarity and brief flowering period. But in Borneo's Gunung Gading National Park, staff usually know when a plant is about to bloom, with November to January the best times to catch them.

© FRANS LANTING / ROBERT HARDING

TAMBOPATA NATIONAL RESERVE, Peru
Thanks to a remarkable level of biodiversity, the Amazon rainforest reserve of Tambopata in southeast Peru is home to 600 species of birds, including the gorgeous scarlet macaw seen here. Thanks to their impressive size — from beak to tail they can be as long as 83cm (33in) — they're easy to spot, whether in Peru or southern Mexico, Bolivia or the Caribbean.

AREQUIPA, Peru
Colourful archways and cloisters abound in the Santa Catalina monastery, one of Peru's most fascinating religious buildings — and one of its biggest. The 2-hectare (5-acre) complex, founded in 1580 by a rich widow, is a citadel within the city. Visit in the evening to see the eerie candlelit interior as entering novices would have done centuries ago.

HONG KONG, China
The contrast between a traditional red sail Chinese junk boat in Victoria Harbour and the surrounding skyscrapers of the city makes for a great experience, especially when the boat is a Chinese wooden sailboat dating back to the Han Dynasty. Few of them remain, and make for a great tour of the harbour or nearby islands.

© SUIWIJA / GETTY IMAGES

© MARKTUCAN / SHUTTERSTOCK

KAKADU NATIONAL PARK, Australia

You could spend a week in the Northern Territory's enormous Kakadu National Park and see all manner of astonishing sights, but the Aboriginal rock art at Ubirr is surely the most majestic. Images include kangaroos, tortoises and fish from around 8000 years ago, but even older are the *mimi* spirits; look out for the yam-head figures, some 15,000 years old.

LA RIOJA, Spain

Miles of dusty, dusky red grapes hang from their vines in Spain's Rioja region, a string of seven valleys a 90-minute drive south of Bilbao. Visiting the hundreds of wineries turning them into fine Riojas makes for a fascinating opportunity to learn about the near-thousand-year history of wine production in the area.

BEIJING, China

In 2020, China celebrates the 600th birthday of its huge Forbidden City, designed as a private imperial palace by a Ming emperor and used until the end of the Quing dynasty in 1912. The anniversary is marked with a section being opened to visitors for the first time ever... though the citadel already offers a full day's worth of exploration without it.

NEW ORLEANS, USA

Cajun cuisine and Louisiana crawfish — aka mudbugs, for the freshwater mud they're found in — are a culinary marriage made in heaven, especially in the crawfish boil. Festivals like Shreveport's Mudbug Madness and the Breaux Bridge Crawfish Festival celebrate the crustacean each May; the rest of the year, try a boil or a seafood po-boy at its best at Seithers Seafood in Harahan.

CUZCO, Peru

The traditional textiles made by Quechua women in the Andes still form a powerful part of their identity. The textiles' history and symbolism — and why the Spanish outlawed their creation and use — are nicely covered at the Centro de Textiles Tradicionales del Cusco, which partners with ten communities from the region to promote this ancient skill.

LIAOHE DELTA, China

The incredible sight of mile upon mile of red beach, 30km (18 miles) southwest of Panjin in Shuangtaizi District, is unforgettable. The red carpet, stretching as far as the eye can see and into the delta, is caused by seepweed, which flowers here between July and October. A combination of bridges, wooden stepping stones and panoramic viewpoints ensure terrific views.

© JAMESBREY / GETTY IMAGES

OREGON, USA

The Painted Hills of the John Day Fossil Beds National Monument In Oregon look for all the world as though some prehistoric giant has splashed vivid stripes of red, yellow, tan, orange, and black paint across this amazing landscape. In winter, colours peak out from patches of melting snow, creating a unique spectacle.

PYONGYANG, North Korea

Each August or September, the Arirang Mass Games In Pyongyang's May Day Stadium take place in front of thousands of spectators. The red colours symbolize the working class and an increasing number of non-Koreans are allowed to watch an eye-popping extravaganza — this is the world's largest gymnastic display, with a record-breaking 100,090 participants in 2007.

BOUDHA, Nepal *(facing page)*

A local woman circles around a prayer wheel at the extraordinary Boudhanath stupa, one of the largest spherical stupas in Nepal and a Unesco World Heritage Site. The wheel lies at the heart of the temple, and as part of Buddhist meditation and karma practice is often turned for hours by a devotee. Visit during Losar (Tibetan New Year) in February or March to experience the largest celebration in Nepal.

ESPELETTE, France

Strings of local chillies, famed for their intensity of aroma rather than heat, dry in front of the red and white Labourd houses of Espelette, near Biarritz in the Basque region of southwest France. The houses' colours are taken from the Basque *ikurrina* flag of red, white and green, though the latter is often provided by nature in the hills and valleys of the region.

© ERIC LAFFORGUE / LONELY PLANET

© JUSTIN FOULKES / LONELY PLANET

TOKYO, Japan

The 90 wooden pillars or gates that make up the Torii Path tunnel at the west entrance to the Shinto Hie Shrine Nagatachō in Chiyoda are its most popular and photographed feature — and are found only at Shinto shrines. The path marks the division between our world and the spirit (*kami*) world; Kyoto's Fushimi Inari Shrine boasts an equally spectacular tunnel.

NORTHERN FORESTS, Sweden

Swedes are keen foragers, and thanks to half of their country being covered in forest and a legally enshrined right of public access, there are plenty of spots for them to do it. In the northern provinces, cowberries (aka lingonberries, red whortleberry or mountain-cranberry) are one of the most popular berries to gather in August and September.

LOFOTEN ISLANDS, Norway

In the Norwegian Lofoten archipelago, the dramatic backdrop of brooding grey peaks such as Svolværgeita and Himmeltindan provides a striking contrast to the hundreds of cute red fishermen's cabins, or *rorbuer*. Why red? Because its mix of ochre with cod liver oil or other animal oil was cheap. Many of the huts are now available to stay in.

MANCHESTER, England

Manchester United's crown may have slipped in recent years, but the club remains enormously popular across the world. In Southeast Asia, where red is associated with good luck, the team are followed by millions. And sights like this one, with thousands of scarves laid out on fans' seats at a cup tie, inspire awe and pride in the hearts of football fans from the red half of the city and beyond.

RED CENTRE, Australia

Australia's Red Centre is aptly named, given its miles of red dust and rocks, all lit up by fiery sunsets. You could spend a week immersed in the colour here, exploring mountain ranges like the West Macs and some of Aboriginal Australia's most sacred sites, including Uluru and the rounded domes of Kata Tjuta, and still not cover it all.

CHRISTMAS ISLAND, Australian Territory

Sir David Attenborough once described the sight of more than a hundred million red crabs swarming across roads, bridges, streams, rocks and beaches to breed in the Indian Ocean as one of his greatest TV moments. And he's had *a lot* of great TV moments. To try and see the great migration for yourself, coincide your arrival with the first rainfall of the wet season.

© WENDY CONNETT / GETTY IMAGES

© MATTHIAS KESTEL / SHUTTERSTOCK

© JUSTIN FOULKES / LONELY PLANET

OAXACA, Mexico
Giant tubs of deep red, deep-fried grasshoppers, or *chapulines*, are a common sight in Oaxaca's vibrant markets, including Mercado Benito Júarez and its neighbour, Mercado 20 de Noviembre. From these protein-rich snacks to vats of *mole* sauces and *huitlacoche* (dried corn fungus), the city is famed as a foodie destination.

GLACIER EXPRESS, Switzerland
A passenger takes in the views on the Bernina Express, or Glacier Express, which regularly appears on top ten lists of best train journeys in the world. From the wraparound windows of the gaily painted red train, spectacular vistas open up as the carriages wind their way through the mountain resorts of Zermatt and St Moritz via Andermatt in the Swiss Alps.

WADI RUM, Jordan
The red dunes and rock formations of southern Jordan's Wadi Rum create a wonderfully moody landscape as the sun cuts through chiselled *siqs* (canyons) at dawn or blurs the division between rock and sand at dusk. Take a day trip from Aqaba or Petra, or spend a night at one of the desert camps to immerse yourself in the experience.

MOSCOW, Russia

The red-brick palace of the State Historical Museum towers opposite St Basil's Cathedral in Red Square. With its distinctive silver-tipped turrets, it's regarded as one of the country's best examples of late 19th-century Russian-style architecture. Inside, it traces the development of Russia and its people from ancient times to the present.

BUÑOL, Spain

Squishy, squelchy and surely the pinnacle of red experiences, Buñol's La Tomatina Festival is probably the most fun its 40,000 participants will ever have with a tomato. If you want to experience the mayhem, head for Valencia in late August; the festival takes place annually on the last Wednesday of the month.

RIO TINTO, Spain

Southwest Spain's Rio Tinto would make a great setting for the mythical Styx, its blood-red and orange colours chillingly evoking the route to Hades. And it's not just the colours that are hellish; a chemical makeup based on centuries of ore mining makes the water extremely acidic and toxic. To see it, follow the river north from the Andalucian town of Niebla.

KHANEQAH, Iran

The ruby-red jewels of pomegranates brighten up market stalls across the Middle East, with many towns ending their harvest with festivals of thanksgiving. In the Iranian village of Khaneqah, in the western province of Kermanshah, celebrating red-clad villagers have lots of them to be thankful for; domestic production of pomegranate exceeds a million tons every year.

HITACHI SEASIDE PARK, Japan

Facing the Pacific Ocean in the city of Hitachinaka, the Hitachi Seaside Park blooms with a rainbow of colourful flowers throughout the year. Perhaps loveliest are the cute pompoms of *kochia* (summer cypress) whose bright green summer hues change to pinky-red then scarlet in autumn, turning to gold by late October.

FLORENCE, Italy *(facing page)*

Rugby, pah. American football, child's play. When it comes to the most brutal team sport in the world, many agree that Florence's historic Calcio Storico tournament, dating from the 16th century and still played each June in clothing from the period, takes the prize. Here, players from teams representing two of the city's four historic districts fight it out for the Chianina heifer.

ALASKA, USA

Wild salmon arrive in spawning grounds at Power Creek, a tributary of Eyak Lake and the Copper River delta near Cordova and Prince William Sound in south central Alaska. Spawning runs from May through September, with king salmon arriving from mid-May to late June, sockeye in May and August, and Coho from late August to September.

ORANGE

© ROBERT FRERCK / ROBERT HARDING

© PATRICIA HOFMEESTER / 500PX

© JUAN CARLOS MUÑOZ ROBREDO / ALAMY STOCK PHOTO

NAZCA DESERT, Peru

Man-made or alien-made? The 300+ Nazca Line drawings of animals, plants and geometric shapes date from 200 BC to 700 AD, which has led to many wild theories about their creators. Composed of lines created by clearing away the darker upper layer to reveal the lighter subsoil, the drawings are only recognisable from on high, ideally in a light aircraft – a hair-raising experience but one that just might make you believe the alien theory.

RIO DE JANEIRO, Brazil

This sunny delight, a golden lion tamarin (or golden marmoset) likes to hang out in the Atlantic coastal forests of its native Brazil, but as an endangered species your chances of seeing it in the wild are slight. If you do want to try your luck, head for the humid forests and keep your chin up: they like to swing among the many vines of the closed canopy, rarely descending lower than 10m (29 ft).

AIT BEN-HADDOU, Morocco

Film fans may recognise the striking Ait-Ben-Haddou from a number of movies, including *Lawrence of Arabia*, *Jewel of the Nile* and *Gladiator*. In truth, little of the original fortified clay casbah remains, but it's a great example of red mud-brick pre-Saharan architecture, dating as far back as the 11th century. Head high above the village to take in its mosque, square and two cemeteries (Muslim and Jewish).

ARIZONA, USA *(previous page)*

The Wave sandstone formations of the Coyote Buttes ravine near the Arizona/Utah borders look like so many giant swirls and whirls of soft-scoop coffee ice cream. The calcified cinnamon-coloured strata apparently induce a drug-like effect on some visitors. Not that there are many: only 20 a day are allowed to walk through the ravine, and permits are required.

PURNULULU NATIONAL PARK, Australia
Better known by the rather cute name of
the Bungle Bungles, the orange-and-black
striped domes of the beehive-shaped karst
sandstone formations rising 250m (820ft)
at Piccaninny Creek turn into a golden
wonder when they're bathed in warm evening
light. It's the formations that are the real star
here, and they're criss-crossed by numerous
walking trails.

KRONG SIEM REAP, Cambodia
A monk walks through temple ruins at Ta
Prohm, famous to non-religious visitors as
the temple from the 2001 *Tomb Raider* and
Indiana Jones and the Temple of Doom. Don't
be fooled by the seemingly natural merging
of jungle and temple; while the building
was indeed abandoned in the 15th century,
its 'neglect' has been carefully managed to
remain stable and accessible.

CHIANG MAI, Thailand
The Yi Peng Festival, more popularly known
as the sky lantern festival, is held each year
in Yi Peng to celebrate and show respect
to Buddha. Its date usually coincides with
Loi Krathong, which the whole country
celebrates with floating lights on water, but
here in Chiang Mai, the lights are also placed
into lanterns and sent skyward to fill the air
with a warm orange glow.

© BIOSPHOTO / ALAMY STOCK PHOTO

BANGALORE, India

Sunshine-bright orange and yellow French marigolds, or *chendu hoovu*, are a feature throughout India, where they're used in marriages and festivals, at temples, and even in salads. So widespread are they that they're grown as far afield as Uttar Pradesh and Karnataka, where drought-hit farmers are turning to them more and more as a reliable and consistently profitable crop.

MUNICH, Germany

If it's September in Bavaria, it's time for beer... lots and lots of beer. At the annual Oktoberfest, held during the second part of the month, literally millions of litres of the amber ale are consumed by some six million devotees, who travel from all over the world to experience this 200-year-old festival of music, food, games and — yep — lots and lots of beer.

ABU SIMBEL, Egypt *(facing page)*

The orange rocks of Abu Simbel are home to some of Egypt's most impressive ancient sights, including four colossi and the Temple of Ramses II. Over five years in the 1960s, in a modern feat of engineering that nicely echoes the 1264 BC one that created the site, the complex was dismantled from its location on the Nile and rebuilt on a desert plateau nearby to make way for the Aswan High Dam.

RANUA, Lapland, Finland

This golden cloudberry is a fleeting and delicate beauty which ripens for a very few short weeks in summer, when midges make hay in the bogs of Finnish Lapland. Due to their delicacy (and those midges) and the fact that they grow just one to a plant, you might not want to join in their harvesting, but at Ranua's Cloudberry Festival, held on the first weekend in August, you can fill up on the fruit.

© KAJEN / SHUTTERSTOCK

© MARK READ / LONELY PLANET

CURONIAN SPIT, Lithuania
Thanks in part to the movie *Jurassic Park*, amber holds a fascination for those of us who love the idea of holding an object that several million years ago was a living thing, namely tree resin, with the chance another living things could be immortalised inside it. Head along the Curonian Spit's 98km (61 miles) of Baltic Sea shoreline to try your hand at finding a piece of your own.

NAMIB NAUKLUFT NATIONAL PARK, Namibia
A springbok surveys its surroundings in front of the large red sand dunes that are a feature of the oldest desert on earth. At its central area of Sossusvlei, dunes rise up more than 300m (984ft), and through the park and neighbouring nature reserve more than 50 species of mammals have been recorded, including oryx, giraffes, African wild cats, aardvarks and reintroduced black rhinos.

KIMBE BAY, Papua New Guinea
The unusual geology of Kimbe Bay's seabed — a mix of volcanoes, mountains, reefs and shelves dropping off into mile-deep waters — makes it one of the world's best places to find marine life. Among 536 types of coral and about 900 species of reef fish, the bright orange clownfish is one of the sweetest, its symbiotic relationship with anemones allowing both to flourish.

MICHOACÁN, Mexico

To see monarch or mariposa butterflies congregating in their millions is a very special experience. It's easy to do too, for each September, they head to southern California and Mexico, where several reserves can be visited, particularly in Michoacán. The week-long Festival Cultural de la Mariposa Monarca takes place at the end of February and beginning of March to coincide with the end of the butterfly season.

DARVAZA, Turkmenistan

Not a volcano but a collapsed natural gas field, the evocatively named Gates of Hell at Darvaza are worth seeing just to tell friends you've been to the gates of hell and back. A controlled (and meant to be temporary) fire lit by geologists more than 40 years ago to prevent the spread of methane gas, it remains an impressive sight.

NEW ENGLAND, USA

Loved by leaf-peepers in the know, the White Mountain National Forest of New Hampshire is just one spot where each autumn the foliage of thousands of trees bursts into reds, oranges and yellows. For the best trails and regularly updated information, check out visit-newhampshire.com/state/foliage/, which lists drives like the 55km (34-mile) Kancamagus Highway, dotted with enough viewing spots to ensure oohs and aahs galore.

SHARQUIY SANDS, Oman
Between Muscat and Sur, the wind-blasted orange contours that make up the dunes of the Wahiba Sands are a treat to visit, and offer a glimpse of a traditional way of life for the 3,000 or so Bedouins who still live as nomads in the ever-shifting sands. Stay overnight in a traditional black-wool tent to get the tiniest sense of life they live here.

CENTRAL SURINAME RESERVE, Suriname
This glorious male Guianan cock-of-the-rock with its delicate silky plumes inhabits various parts of the vast Central Suriname nature reserve, but head for Raleighvallen (Raleigh Falls) on the upper Coppename River and you should have no problem finding the rooster-sized bird in its lek (a kind of performance court). Climb the nearby Voltzberg granite dome for fabulous 360-degree jungle views.

IVREA, Italy
Spain's Buñol has its Tomatina (see p23), but how would it fare in a battle with Italy's Ivrea, where a highlight of the annual three-day Ivrea Festival is the Battle of the Oranges? Reenacting a 12th-century clash, *aranceri* (the people, on foot) exchange fruity firepower with Napoleonic troops, in carts. We can't help feeling the oranges' superior weight and heft would paste the Spanish tomato tossers.

© C&E2010 / SHUTTERSTOCK

VATICAN CITY, Italy

Illuminated by its glorious gold ceiling, the walls of the Gallery of Maps at the Vatican Museum are a cartography fan's delight, filled as they are with 40 16th-century painted topographical maps of Italy based on drawings by cosmographer and geographer Ignazio Danti. The impressive works form the world's largest series of painted maps.

AMSTERDAM, The Netherlands

Dutch revellers fill Amsterdam's canals, bridges, streets, parks and squares to celebrate King's Day, or Konningsdag, on 27 April. It's not an old tradition, having replaced Queen's Day, or Koninginnedag, in 2014, but the festivities are unchanged as seemingly everyone in Amsterdam dresses head to toe in orange to celebrate their royal family.

BAGAN, Myanmar

The North Guni Temple is just one of some 4000 red-brick temples and stupas that fill the plain of Bagan. Until 2018, cycling through the pre-dawn light to climb the larger temples, with the vast plain below bathed in growing gold by the light of the rising sun, was quite likely to bring on a bout of Stendhal Syndrome; nowadays, a hot-air balloon ride might do the same, albeit for a lot more money.

© MATT MUNRO / LONELY PLANET

© NISANGHA / GETTY IMAGES

TOKYO, Japan

In a sea of steel and concrete towers, the bright orange-and-white striped Tokyo Tower stands out like the beacon it is, as this aerial view of metropolitan Tokyo and the communications and observation tower shows. To get the view shown here, head to the 238m (780ft) high Sky Deck of the Mori Tower, where the open-air viewing platform affords a 360° view of the whole Greater Tokyo region.

WOODSTOCK, USA

Pumpkins arranged in rows to be hardened off and dried are a growing feature across New York state and the wider US, particularly Illinois. This Midwestern state of pumpkin patches and farms produces an estimated 318 million pounds of the bright orange gourds a year, and attracts thousands of visitors, most of them of course in the market for a car-full to take home for Halloween.

ROUSSILLON, France *(facing page)*

The flame-coloured landscape around Roussillon is a treat to explore, its ochre deposits creating a rich palette of tones along the Sentier des Ocres walking trail, which winds its way among arresting formations and colours and is easily accessible from the village. Come in the late afternoon or early evening to see the setting sun set the surrounding landscape ablaze with colour.

HVERIR, Iceland

You become aware of your growing proximity to the plopping, farting pools of mud and steaming fumaroles at Hverir before you're anywhere near them — or your nose does. Emitting stinky sulfuric gas with a nausea-inducing intensity, it's not a place to linger. But it's worth it; that cracked, orangy-red landscape looks for all the world like another planet entirely — probably Mars.

YELLOW

© CLICKALPS / AWL IMAGES

© IMAGEBROKER / ALAMY STOCK PHOTO

© JULIEN CRUCIANI / ALAMY STOCK PHOTO

NANDGAON, India

Holi brings massed March madness to communities across India, but in the Uttar Pradesh villages of Nandgaon and Barsana, things get really crazy. During Lathmar Holi, men from Nandgaon, in retaliation for teasing the women of Barsana, are driven out with bamboo sticks in a recreation of an event from Lord Krishna's life — and everyone, of course, gets covered in paint.

IZAMAL, Mexico

Yucatán's Izamal is famed for its bright yellow buildings, the most impressive of which is this enormous Franciscan monastery, the Convento de San Antonio de Padua, standing at the heart of *la ciudad amarilla* (the yellow city). The 16th-century colonial building uses stones from a Maya temple, the Ppapp-Hol-Chac pyramid, destroyed by the conquering Spanish.

LANGUEDOC-ROUSSILLON, France

Basking in the valleys between the Pyrenees and the Alps, western Provence and Languedoc-Roussillon offer sunflowers as far as the eye can see. The rolling hills south of Castelnaudary are a prime spot in which to surround yourself with field upon field of the nodding 'turn around the suns', as their name in French, *tournesol*, literally translates.

TRINIDAD, Cuba *(previous page)*

Cuba's music scene is legendary — and legendarily colourful. Once you've soaked up some of the vibrant sounds and sights on the street, let your eyes and ears feast on the good-time vibes at the country's iconic music venues, among them Havana jazz club La Zorra y El Cuervo and Casa de la Musica in kaleidoscopic Trinidad.

TUAMOTUS ISLANDS, French Polynesia
This cute critter, named the longhorn cowfish for its protruding horns and featuring a yellow body with white spots, is an easy one to spot in shallow coral lagoons and estuaries as far afield as the Red Sea and Australia. Adventurous divers could head for one of the 77 atolls that make up the Tuamotus Islands, the largest chain of atolls in the world.

DAR EL JELD, Tunisia
Pass through the bee-yellow front door in this 18th-century mansion and a magnificent courtyard dining space is theatrically revealed. Great local specialities include *sebnekhia* (octopus with beans and spinach) and *kabkabou* (fish and tomato stew). For a more mellow yellow taste of the capital, Tunis, head to the nearby locals' favourite beaches of La Marsa and La Goulette.

PORT OF SPAIN, Trinidad & Tobago
Whether it's Rara in Haiti, Mardi Gras in New Orleans or Carnaval in Cuba and Brazil, carnival is party time, and party time requires a suitably eye-catching party dress. These days, costumes are mostly glorified bikinis with beads and feathers, but at mas camps in Trinidad, ladies still gather each winter to hand-make elaborate, intricate outfits such as this one.

TIGRAY, Ethiopia

A monk climbs up to a small cave in the cliff-face leading to the famous Debre Damo monastery. Reaching it makes for a memorable experience (for men, at least — women aren't allowed up), involving the ascent of a sheer 15m (49ft) cliff using a leather rope. Some of the 150 yellow-clad monks living in the monastery are usually on hand to help out.

SINTRA, Portugal

The arresting Pena Palace in Sintra, built in Portugal in the 19th century as the summer residence of the royal family, sits magnificently on a rocky outcrop. The vibrant colours of the palace's original exterior were restored in 1996, and on a clear day it can be easily seen from Lisbon and much of the capital's metropolitan area.

BOLSA CHICA RESERVE, USA *(facing page)*

Not seen in the open very often, but common throughout the year in the Bolsa Chica Ecological Reserve at California's Huntington Beach, a male common yellowthroat warbler perches among yellow wild mustard flowers. Birdwatchers will thrill to the trill of the reserve's other 185 regularly occurring species, with 116 less frequently seen species.

AMALFI, Italy

The 'sfusato Amalfitano' lemons hanging on vertiginous terraced groves are an iconic symbol of Campania's Amalfi and Sorrento. The result of small traditional lemons crossed with local bitter oranges in the 11th century, these knobbly beasts are sweet enough (just) to be eaten as fruit, but taste way better in the local hooch, the famous limoncello.

DALLOL, Ethiopia

Springs of acid bring vibrant colours to the world's hottest spot, Dallol in Ethiopia's Danakil Depression. Steaming yellow sulphur fields malodorously dot a salt basin that's 116m (380ft) below sea level in places, making it the lowest dry point on earth. It's best visited from November to March, when temperatures drop below their average of 34.4°C (94°F).

COMMERCY, France

That quintessential cake of literary fans the world over, Marcel Proust's famous honey-yellow memory trigger is still made in the traditional way at La Boîte à Madeleines in the Lorraine region's Commercy, where large-scale production of the buttery shell-shaped sponge is said to have begun more than 250 years ago.

TANNERON, France

Other parts of France may laud bigger and brasher yellow flowers, but in the village of Tanneron, just 24km (15 miles) from Cannes, it's all about the mimosa. As home to the largest mimosa forest in Europe, the area bursts with colour each February, thanks to the plant's introduction from Australia for use in the perfume industry at nearby Grasse.

JAISALMER FORT, India
From miles around, the sight of the tawny-coloured Jaisalmer Fort, built using the local Jurassic sandstone, looks for all the world like a golden (and very elaborate) sandcastle rising from the sandy expanse of western Rajasthan. But this is no temporary sandcastle; some 3000 people live within the Sonar Quila, or Golden Fort.

CARRIZO PLAIN NATIONAL MONUMENT, USA
A super bloom, as seen here on California's Carrizo Plain, is an amazing sight, especially if you come expecting to see the valley in its typical arid and dusty state. Goldfields, tidy tips, hillside daisies and desert dandelions are just some of the blooms that can turn the plain into a golden spring carpet after heavy autumn or winter rains.

MANYARA NATIONAL PARK, Tanzania
These Little Bee Eaters are just two of the stars in the small but underrated Manyara National Park, which, thanks to 11 ecosystems across lakes, savannah, marshland, acacia woodlands, evergreen forests and dramatic escarpments, is a twitchers' heaven. Come during the rain to see millions of flamingos and other bird life.

ROTTERDAM, The Netherlands
Piet Blom's 1970s tilted cube houses are as weird to live in as they are to take in, with their walls and windows all angled at 54.7 degrees. According to their designer, the houses are meant to represent trees which, taken together, become a man-made yellow forest. A Show Cube Museum and Stayokay hostel offer the chance to peek inside.

PACIFIC COAST, Colombia
Small — most are just 3–4cm (1–2 inches) long — but utterly deadly, this golden poison dart frog, endemic to the Pacific coast of Colombia, can kill 10 people with a single dose of its venom. Canny indigenous cultures such as the Chocó have been dipping their blow darts in the frogs' poison for centuries — hence their common name.

MEKNES, Morocco
The Mausoleum of Moulay Ismail is a tour de force of Moroccan craftsmanship befitting a sultan whose family were descendants of the Prophet Muhammad. It has been under restoration since 2016, and when it emerges it should look extra special; in the meantime, the town's winding narrow medina streets and grand buildings are worth a visit in their own right.

© MARCO BOTTIGELLI / AWL IMAGES LTD

LOWER SAXONY, Germany
Windbreak, beach chair, parasol and umbrella all in one… the ultra-utilitarian *strandkorb* bathing seat was invented in 1882 by German basket maker Wilhelm Bartelmann. The seats come in all colours along the seafront resorts of Lower Saxony; these yellow lovelies reside at the North Sea resort of Duhnen, near Cuxhaven.

NAMBURG NATIONAL PARK, Australia
The Pinnacles Desert in Namburg National Park near Perth is a jaw-dropping sight, its thousands of limestone pillars and columns thrusting up from a stark landscape of yellow sand to form one of Western Australia's most intriguing landscapes. During September and October, wildflowers add bold splashes of other colours to the mix.

NEW YORK, USA
As much a part of the cityscape as the skyscrapers they pass in their thousands, an estimated 13,5000 NY taxi cabs form a near-constant sea of yellow movement up and down Manhattan's streets. Catch them while you can — ride-hailing apps and congestion charging are putting them under threat of extinction.

© SCOTT THISTLETHWAITE / GETTY IMAGES

© PESKYMONKEY / GETTY IMAGES

LUXOR, Egypt

The ancient site of Luxor and the Karnak temple complex are truly mind-blowing, especially when you think of how much work went into constructing the yellow-rock site. The Hypostyle Hall is the apotheosis of it, a vast area studded with 134 massive columns stretching up as high as 21m (69ft), bearing architraves estimated to weigh 63 tonnes (69 tons).

TOKYO, Japan *(facing page)*

Vibrant natural attractions are celebrated in style in Japan, and the Jingu Gaien Ginkgo Festival, held from mid-November to early December, is no exception. The golden autumn leaves falling from an avenue of 150 ginko trees form a glorious 300m (984ft) long carpet leading to a festival site offering regional dishes from the whole country.

RAIN FORESTS, Madagascar

The intriguing moon moth, also known as a comet moth, has a impressive wingspan of 20cm (8in), making it one of the world's largest silk moths. Your chances of seeing it are pretty slim; it lives for a week at most, and despite its long tail, is well camouflaged during its short life in its native Madagascan rain forests.

LISBON, Portugal

The Glória Funicular or Elevador da Glória is a must-do in the city – not least because the alternative, walking, is a real slog. Connecting Restauradores Square downtown with Rua San Pedro de Alcántara in Bairro Alto, it's the most popular of the city's three funiculars for tourists, perhaps because the views from the top are so outstanding.

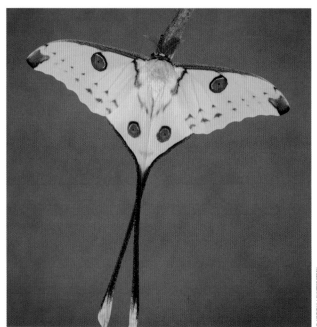

© MARIAN GALOVIC / SHUTTERSTOCK

© MATT ANDERSON PHOTOGRAPHY / GETTY IMAGES

© SUSAN WRIGHT / LONELY PLANET

HOI AN, Vietnam

A local woman in a *non la* palm-leaf conical hat rides past the traditional yellow houses lining the river banks of Hoi An. Follow her example by hiring a bike, grabbing a *banh mi* (sandwich) and exploring the wonderful golden-yellow buildings — just some of the 844 ancient Unesco World Heritage listed houses — in this beguiling city.

GRAND TETON NATIONAL PARK, USA

Aspen groves in autumnal yellows, with the snow-covered peaks of the Grand Tetons behind them, make for a spectacular sight on the hillsides of Wyoming's Grand Teton National Park. Years of experience have taught fans that the third week in September is usually peak golden wonder week.

BOLOGNA, Italy

Bologna and Modena still fight it out over the invention of Italy's famed tortellini, but in the city known as *la grassa* (the fat), there's no disputing the exquisite shapes and tastes of the little filled dumplings. Try them in *brodo* (broth) at Trattoria Gianni, or buy them to take home in gorgeous packaging at Bolognese pasta store Paolo Atti e Figli.

MIAMI, USA

When fans of classic 20th-century architecture come to Miami, they head for one area: South Beach. Filled with some 800 fine examples of pastel art deco designs from the 1930s and 40s, the sleek, streamlined, iridescent buildings between 5th Street to the south and Dade Boulevard to the north makes for a wonderfully theatrical streetscape.

YUNNAN, China

Spring bursts into sunny colour in the fields of the Yunnan province of Luoping. Each year from February to March, 8 hectares (20 acres) of floral splendour form the heart of the Canola Flower Festival, with Luosi field in north and Jinji Peak in the south offering the most picturesque spots.

TORTUGUERO NATIONAL PARK, Costa Rica

More famous for the sea turtles that give the national park its name, Tortuguero is home to a large number of other docile critters, like the endangered West Indian manatee, and some more deadly ones, like this yellow eyelash viper, named for the striking superciliary scales above its eyes.

© PIO.DE / GETTY IMAGES

© TANES NGAMSOM / GETTY IMAGES

© KEVIN WELLS PHOTOGRAPHY / SHUTTERSTOCK

GREEN

© MILAN ZYGMUNT / SHUTTERSTOCK

© RALF-FINN HESTOFT / GETTY IMAGES

© MARCO MACCARINI / GETTY IMAGES

KGALAGADI TRANSFRONTIER PARK, Botswana & South Africa

The green African bullfrog is surely the model for *The Frog Prince* – you half expect to see a little crown on its head. But you wouldn't want to test out the kissing theory; it has sharp teeth and bites humans when provoked. And it's big – up to 23cm (9in) – which should make it pretty easy to find in the 38,000sq km (15,000 sq miles) of the Kgalagadi reserve.

KAMAKURA, Japan

The sound of the wind in a bamboo grove is otherwordly, and to hear it here in the seaside town of Kamakura's Hokokuji Temple is a deeply moving experience. The 2000 moso bamboos lie just behind the temple's main hall, which houses an impressive Buddha beyond the Zen temple gate. Kyoto's Arashiyama grove is equally enchanting, as is the Sagano Scenic Railway route to it – also known as the Sagano Romantic Train.

CHICAGO, USA

For more than 50 years, on the morning of Chicago's St Patrick's Day Parade, the city's river has been dyed green by the same two families using 18kg (40 pounds) of dye pellets. The effect only lasts for a few hours and takes place between Columbus Drive and State Street in a tradition only broken once; to celebrate the Cubs winning the World Series in 2016, the river was turned a brilliant blue.

MACHU PICCHU, Peru *(previous page)*

Way up high in the Andes, hidden by mist, lush vegetation and steep escarpments, the plateau on which Machu Picchu sat undetected by the conquering Spaniards was only discovered in 1911. Thus, 600 years after it was built, we can explore every inch of the citadel's well-preserved temples, palaces, plazas, tombs, water distribution systems and houses, awed by the achievements of the 15th-century Incas who built it.

PADANG PADANG, Bali

There's something for everyone at Bali's Padang Padang beach, which, like most beaches in Uluwatu, is famous for consistent surf that ranges from beginners' breaks on the right to the more tricky left-hand point, often used for surfing competitions. Back on land, watch out for the hordes of thieving monkeys massed along the picturesque staircase in the limestone cliff-face.

MUONIO, Finland

The trick with going anywhere to see the northern lights, or aurora borealis, is to choose somewhere you'll enjoy even if the lights don't shine. Muonio, near the border between Finland and Sweden, is one such place, as is Norway's Tromsø, in the middle of the auroral oval, the area with the highest probability of seeing the lights. Aim for September to April and keep your fingers crossed.

BERLIN, Germany

The five copper domes and several copper statues, all of them with a bright verdigris patina, are the main feature of the Berliner Dom, or Berlin Cathedral Church. While the current church dates from just 1905, the copper roofs, resistant to corrosion in most environments, can theoretically last 1000 years. Climb the 270 stairs up the dome for great city views.

SAN GERARDO DE DOTA, Costa Rica

The aptly named green violetear hummingbird, or Mexican violetear, is just one of the colourful reasons birdwatchers come to San Gerardo de Dota, in the high mountain valleys of the Talamanca mountain range. The others are some 200 other bird species — including the stunning quetzal — that inhabit a region filled with mountain lodges and some excellent trekking.

QUEENSLAND, Australia

Was the arboreal green tree python the inspiration behind *The Jungle Book*'s nasally challenged Kaa? They certainly behave alike, with their habit of looping coils over tree branches and placing their head in the middle. As the name suggests, the adult snake is a vibrant green, but juvenile snakes vary in colour from red, orange, and yellow to dark brown–black, all in the same clutch.

WAIKATO, New Zealand *(facing page)*

Literally nestled within the rolling hills around Matamata, the Hobbiton movie set, about a 45-minute drive from the city of Hamilton, is filled with the facades of hobbit homes like this one, used for the *Lord of the Rings* and *Hobbit* films. The gently bucolic landscape was felt to be a perfect visualisation of JRR Tolkien's Shire, which was constructed a year before shooting began on the movies.

ÖRÆFI, Iceland

Blanketed in a verdant turf roof, Hofskirkja Church is a great example of a tradition that goes back to the 9th century, when Iceland's first turf dwellings arrived with Norse settlers, who replaced hard-to-find timber with plentiful turf as the primary material for their buildings. Its insulating, renewable and durable properties have ensured its continuing use centuries on.

VÍK, Iceland

A lone hiker takes in the dramatic landscape inland from Vík, the southernmost village in Iceland. Mýrdalsjökull Glacier, at 1,493m (4,898ft), is just one of the amazing hiking routes in the area; the basalt columns of the Dyrhólaey peninsula, arresting red and white Reyniskirkja Church, and puffins nesting in the cliffs of Reynisfjall mountain are some more reasons to spend time here.

PADRÓN, Spain

Beware. This portion of mild *pimientos de Padrón*, by the laws of probability (10–25%), going to include at least a few eye-wateringly hot ones. It's a peculiarity of the variety, native to Padrón near Santiago de Compostela in Galicia, There is of course a festival, held each August in nearby Herbón, at which for a few euros a plate can be refilled with the freshly fried salty treats as many times as you want. And you get to keep the plate as a souvenir.

NEW YORK, USA

The most iconic copper-covered edifice in the world gazes implacably out, perhaps safe in the knowledge that while her 'tired, poor, huddled masses' will come and go with the decades, she will remain serene and safe under her hundred-ton layer of near-pure copper and its protective verdigris patina, as she has done since her originally brown form of 1886 acquired its oxidised coat.

TUSCANY, Italy

Rolling hills blanketed in bright green fields, spiked with elegant farmhouses and cypress trees that rise from hazy morning mists . . . it can only be Tuscany. The verdant landscape of rural estates growing everything from grapes and olives to grains and orchard fruits never fails to disappoint, and stunning towns and cities like Pisa, Lucca, Siena, Maremma and Florence complete the very special appeal.

VERMONT, USA

Rising high above the treeline in the Green Mountains, the famous white steeple of Stowe Community Church is visible for miles around. The town, filled with 19th-century historical buildings, is a magnet in autumn and winter, when people come in their thousands to admire the fall colours of the region, and ski the nearby slopes of Mount Mansfield.

MASHAM, England

For almost a century, dried hops from Yorkshire and the rest of the UK have been used to make beer in the Yorkshire Dales market town of Masham, where six-generation-old brewery T&R Theakston uses traditional kit and methods of production to create winsomely named ales such as Old Peculier, Barista Stout, Hurly Burly Brew and, ahem, Cooper's Butt.

© DANITA DELIMONT / ALAMY STOCK PHOTO

© JUSTIN FOULKES / LONELY PLANET

© PAVELSINITCYN / GETTY IMAGES

ZAANDAM, The Netherlands

The restored Poelenburg windmill of the Zaanse Schans open-air museum is a big draw in Zaandam. Stay at the Hotel Inntel Zaandam; designed by architect Wilfried van Winden, its 70 cottage facades stacked on top of each other were inspired by the small cottages of the region and Claude Monet's painting *The Blue House at Zaandam*.

BOHOL, Philippines

More than a thousand rounded mounds spread across the province of Bohol, creating the enchanting landscape of the Chocolate Hills, a geological curiosity filling an area of more than 50 sq km (31 sq miles). There's nothing edible about them: the hills' name is derived from the way their green turf turns brown during the dry season. See them at their most magical from the viewing platform in Carmen town.

HAYFIELD, England

The village of Hayfield has one of the most beautiful settings in England. Surrounded by the verdant fields and hills of the Peak District, it has been here since the Doomsday Book, when it was called 'Hedfeld' and was a natural clearing in the vast forest at the foot of Kinder Scout, the highest point in the Peak District.

SHANGHAI, China
Shanghai is home to millions of green postboxes, some of which are famous. On the corner of Zhongshan Dong Yi Road and Hankou Road, pop star Lu Han's pose next to the box led to queues of teenage fans wanting to follow suit, while loved-up couples head for the box on Tian'ai Road, whose name means 'sweet love'. A letter posted here gets a special 'love' stamp on it.

HASTINGS, England
Traditional May Day celebrations such as Morris dancing are taken to a new level in Hastings, East Sussex, where the four-day Jack in the Green May Day festival marking the beginning of summer culminates with a parade featuring hundreds of elaborately decorated pagan figures waiting to slay the foliage-covered Jack in the Green.

HANGZHOU, China
Stunning views of bright green tea fields aren't hard to find in China, which, combined with India, supplied 62% of the world's tea in 2016. But tea fields you can experience close-up are a little harder to access. Hangzhou bucks the trend with the tourist-friendly Long Jing (Dragon Well) Tea Plantation, where steep hill terraces of tea plants create a mesmerising landscape.

ST PETERSBURG, Russia

The vibrant facade of St Petersburg's Winter Palace identifies it as part of one of the world's most famous museums, the State Hermitage (see p129). Replete with gold and white columns and classical statues, it has survived two centuries of revolution and shifting architectural fashions virtually unchanged but for its colour — it was painted its distinctive green after WWII.

TONGARIRO NATIONAL PARK, New Zealand

The impossibly green volcanic lakes of this arresting landscape are just one highlight of the Tongariro Alpine Crossing, which offers steaming vents and springs, stunning rock formations, peculiar moonscape basins, seriously tricky scree slopes and vast views. No wonder it's often cited as the best one-day walk in New Zealand.

COCA, Ecuador *(facing page)*

An aerial view of the brown Napo river snaking through the green jungle of the Ecuadorian Amazon. At a total length of 1075km (668 miles), travelling along it from Coca in Ecuador to Iquitos in Peru offers a memorable experience that, intrepid travellers claim, can be done using four boats in four days — erratic timetables, mosquitoes, snakes and piranha allowing.

LONDON, England

The lush rainforest plants crowding the iconic Palm House of Kew Gardens are best viewed from the wrought iron walkway of the 19m (62ft) high central nave, which affords a rare view of tree crowns. Built in 1844, the design borrowed techniques from the ship-building industry — which might explain why it resembles the upturned hull of a ship.

BLUE

© MARK READ / LONELY PLANET

© PETER ADAMS / GETTY IMAGES

© MICHAEL RUNKEL / ROBERT HARDING

ISTANBUL, Turkey
Named for divine wisdom (*sophos* in Greek),
the magnificent 1500-year-old Byzantine
Hagia Sophia, or Aya Sofya, was indeed
built — first as a church in 537, converted to
a mosque by Mehmet the Conqueror in 1453
and declared a museum by Atatürk in 1935
— using a great degree of wisdom on the
part of the architects, who worked out how to
balance its 30m (98ft) dome on hidden pillars.

ERG CHEBBI, Morocco
Crossing the Sahara is no small undertaking,
so along with camels and water, your clothing
can be a very important aid to survival. Which
is partly why this Tuareg man is shrouded
in indigo blue, including the *tagelmust*
turban and veil. Helping to protect him from
the sands, wind and heat, the headwear
is exclusive to Tuareg males on reaching
maturity.

WESTLAND TAI POUTINI NP, New Zealand
Tourists hike above a giant crack on Fox
Glacier in Westland Tai Poutini National Park.
Featuring snow-capped mountains, glaciers,
forests, grasslands, lakes, rivers, wetlands
and beaches, it's a landscape that's perfect
for all kinds of outdoor pursuits, including
a 5hr-climb with spectacular views of the
mountains reflected in Lake Gault.

LIGHTHOUSE REEF, Belize *(previous page)*
This beautiful aerial view of the circular
Great Blue Hole, a giant marine sinkhole near
Lighthouse Reef, around 100km (62 miles)
off the coast of Belize, is only bettered by
the view divers get from its 124m (410ft)
depths — and in particular, about a third of
the way down, where the otherwordly marine
stalactites are as long as 15m (50ft).

BUDAPEST, Hungary

If you only sample one of the 50 spas, baths and pools in the City of Spas, make it the vast 1913 neo-baroque Szechenyi Baths, housing 18 pools and ten saunas and steam chambers. If you're a chess fan find the corner of the main bath where the locals play each day, and don't miss the giant outdoor spiral whisk — just follow the shrieks of laughter to find it.

TAFRAOUTE, Morocco

Are they art or a blight on the natural beauty of the red desertscape? The jury's out, but Belgian artist Jean Vérame's bizarrely beautiful blue, red, purple and black *pierres bleues* (blue stones) are clearly appreciated by the local villagers, who have regularly been giving the rocks a fresh coat of paint since Vérame spray-painted them in 1984.

GALÁPAGOS ISLANDS, Ecuador

The natural world is full of smile-inducing delights, and the blue-footed booby is surely one of them. Stomping around in an ungainly mating ritual to show off the size and bright colour of his feet (females have darker ones), the booby's name is particularly apt when he's tottering around on land during the breeding season of June and August.

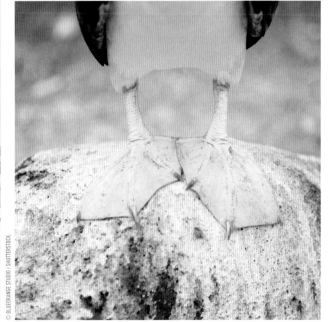

NAXOS, Greece
Nothing evokes the Cyclades more than sunlit blue and white buildings such as the Eggares Olive Press museum. Naxos offers plenty of the sugar-cube buildings (the blue-domed church in Melanes is a highlight), but also medieval Venetian mansions, lots of great hiking — Mount Zas, the highest point in the Cyclades, is a must — and a much quieter experience than you'll find on other islands.

REYKJAVÍK, Iceland
The milky hues of Iceland's Blue Lagoon geothermal spa, with warm water supplied by the nearby Svartsengi geothermal power station. Set in black lava fields just a 30-minute drive from Reykjavík, it makes for an arresting experience — particularly on a winter's evening, when you might be lucky enough to see a northern lights show.

TAHITI, French Polynesia
Australian surfer Jack Robinson tries out the famous break at Teahupoo in Tahiti, French Polynesia. Coral atolls surrounding the island make for great surf and waves here can reach as much as 7m (23ft). Be warned, this is a not a surf spot for the inexperienced; pro surfers have died here, and it's often cited as one of the most dangerous breaks in the world.

GREAT BARRIER REEF, Australia *(facing page)*
Rising ocean temperatures are taking their toll on the coral of the world's largest marine park, which stretches more than 2300km (1430 miles) along Australia's northeast coast. If you visit, make sure to do so via a certified high-standard marine tour operator. A good starting point is in Cairns, where you'll find heaps of options.

© SILENTWINGS / SHUTTERSTOCK

JODHPUR, India

Rajasthan is awash with vibrant colour, and no more so than in the ancient city of Jodhpur, famous for the pastel-blue buildings of its old town. The distinctive blue wash used on so many of the city's 15th-century buildings is best seen from the Mehrangarh Fort; from its hilltop vantage point, the pastel hues are laid out like a patchwork quilt.

MARETTIMO, Italy

The famous blue grottos of Capri and Taormina (the latter featured in Luc Besson's *The Big Blue*) are mesmerising, but often filled with tourists. Under the radar at the other end of Sicily, the Egadi archipelago offers equally glittering prizes in its many submerged caves — Marettimo alone has 400 below and above the water, with one, the Grotta del Cammello, illuminated by a natural skylight.

VATNAJÖKULL, Iceland *(facing page)*

The shifting ice caves of Vatnajökull in southeast Iceland are quite an experience, with perhaps the best one to be had inside the brilliant blue Breiðamerkurjökull (or Crystal Cave). Access, only permitted from November to March, is very weather-dependent, and can be dangerous, so book a good glacier guide and take the necessary safety gear before making the trip.

OXFORD, England

The beguiling Ashmolean is, as you'd expect of the University of Oxford's museum of art and archaeology, filled with treasures from around the globe. This one, a lapis lazuli star of the galleries of Ancient Egypt and Sudan, dates back to around 3300—3000 BC and glistens with intensity and unique features — like the short, tightly curled hair on a head found eight years after her body.

© MASSAMPH / GETTY IMAGES

© HERITAGE IMAGE PARTNERSHIP LTD / ALAMY STOCK PHOTO

© JOHN BRACEGIRDLE / ALAMY STOCK PHOTO

MARRAKESH, Morocco

Away from the chaos and winding alleyways of Marrakesh's medina, the Jardin Majorelle is literally an oasis of cool beauty, its electric blue structural elements beautifully complementing the 300 plant species from five continents. Established by French artist Jacques Majorelle in the 1920s, its existence today is due to Yves Saint Laurent and Pierre Bergé, who bought it in the 1980s.

ESFAHAN, Iran

The 17th-century Sheikh Lotf Allah Mosque, featuring elaborate calligraphy of Quranic verses and multicoloured mosaics on its walls and dome. Inside, the main dome is dominated by a peacock enhanced by changing light through the day. The exterior of this Unesco World Heritage Site, with its intricate decoration and predominance of blue and gold, is just as spectacular.

HITACHI SEASIDE PARK, Japan *(facing page)*

Come in autumn and you'll see the Hitachi Seaside Park aflame in pom-poms of *kochia* (see p24), but in springtime, the same space blooms with 4.5 million azure nemophila, or 'baby blue eyes' flowers, turning the landscape into a stunning canvas of green and pale blues. The sprawling park's Miharashi no Oka ('Lookout Hill') is the place to head, ideally around early May.

LONDON, England

The sweeping Tulip Stairs staircase with its pretty cobalt-blue balustrade is one of the original features of a house built for a queen — the wife of James I — who sadly didn't live to use them. Designed by Inigo Jones, the house featured this self-supporting spiral staircase, the first of its kind in Britain. Now an art gallery, it's part of Greenwich's National Maritime Museum.

© TUNART / GETTY IMAGES

© COWARD_LION / ALAMY STOCK PHOTO

© ANDREA RICORDI / GETTY IMAGES

© KLAUS ULRICH MUELLER / SHUTTERSTOCK

© ROBERTHARDING / ALAMY STOCK PHOTO

CHEFCHAOUEN, Morocco

The striking blue–washed facades of Chefchouen's old–town buildings make it one of the prettiest towns in Morocco — and it's one of the most arty too. Leatherwork and weaving are practised in the workshops lining the steep cobbled lanes, and the old medina is a delight of Moroccan and Andalusian influence. The setting, beneath the peaks of the Rif, is perfect too.

PATAGONIA, Chile

The Marble Caves, or Marble Cathedral, are one of Patagonia's most stunning natural wonders. The colours of the minerals in the caves are spectacular, and the turquoise water, throwing an ethereal blue hue over the sculpted forms and textured walls, creates a memorable sight. Take a boat out onto General Carrera Lake to take it all in.

TUMUCUMAQUE MOUNTAINS PARK, Brazil

You'll have to hunt hard to find this blue poison dart frog, a tiny creature that likes to make its home under leaves, logs and rocks on the forest floor. On the plus side, it's diurnal, which means it's active during the day, but at an average 3cm (1 inch) in length, in the 38,800km sq km (14,980 sq miles) national park, chances of finding it might be slim.

COLORADO, USA

Most airports go for the obvious when commissioning art; generally, things related to flight. Denver instead opted for this fibreglass blue mustang, nicknamed Blucifer both for its glowing red eyes and the fact that it killed its creator Luis Jiménez when a section of it fell on him at his studio in 2006. As a representation of the spirit of the old American west, sculpture doesn't come much wilder.

BANFF NATIONAL PARK, Canada

If you want to see this $20 view of Lake Moraine (literally; it was used on the $20 bills Canada issued between 1969 and 1979) you'll need to time your arrival in the Valley Of The Ten Peaks carefully. Too soon after the road opens in May and it might be frozen under a layer of snow, but in July or August this is the astonishing colour you'll be greeted with — at least until October.

WAIPU CAVE, New Zealand

The so-called glowworm cathedral at the far end of Waipu Cave is an ethereal delight. Access to the glowworm site can be tricky, especially as you navigate the initially pitch-black interior, where plenty of mud and water take the place of paths or tracks, but persevere to the third chamber to see the galaxy of milky-blue pin-pricks illuminating the magical limestone formations.

PORTO, Portugal

Porto's ornate Capela das Almas regularly crops up in lists of the city's most famous churches, thanks to its glorious blue and white azulejo-clad facade. The church dates from the early 18th century, but the tiled panels of scenes from the life and deaths of St Francis of Assisi and St Catherine were only added in 1929, though painted in an 18th-century style to match the architecture.

TULUM, Mexico

The area around Tulum in Mexico's Yucatán is dotted with *cenotes*, or sinkholes, that make perfect swimming and diving spots on a hot day exploring Mayan ruins. Beneath its initially murky surface, this one, the Car Wash or Aktun Ha, reveals gnarly tree roots, lilies, turtles and sometimes a small resident crocodile. Gran Cenote nearby leads to the world's second-largest cave system.

JUKKASJÄRVI, Sweden *(facing page)*

This Long Hall with its table and a chandelier made of ice form one of the main spaces of the Jukkasjärvi's ICEHOTEL. Made of ice and snow, its unheated standard rooms (with temperatures of −5 to −8°C, 41 to 46°F) are only open in winter, but a permanent space enables year-round accommodation if you want to visit in the summer months — though we can't help feeling that's cheating.

PORT OF SPAIN, Trinidad & Tobago

Hours before partying proper takes over the streets of Trinidad, blue or black painted *jab jabs* (blue devils) come out of the pre-dawn darkness to see in J'Ouvert, the early morning opening of Carnival celebrations. If you want to see them, be prepared to be included in their exuberant revelry — and to be covered in the oil, mud, cocoa and paint they'll be liberally throwing around.

PURPLE

© NICK GARBUTT / NATURE PICTURE LIBRARY

© MARK GREEN / ALAMY STOCK PHOTO

© WERNER VAN STEEN / GETTY IMAGES

EL PAUJIL NATURE RESERVE, Colombia
The Paujil Nature Reserve is special not just for being home to this scarily large — its average length is 19cm (7.5in) — Colombian Purple Bloom spider, but because it's the first protected area in the Magdalena Valley, an area once rich in biodiversity and endemic species now threatened by large-scale deforestation.

PROVENCE, France
Famed for lavender fields stretching away to the hazy horizon, the perfume of Provence is an irresistable summer scent during June and July. To see it at its most ethereally beautiful head for Avignon and the fields around the elegant Cistercian Abbey of Notre-Dame de Senanque, near the picture-perfect hilltop village of Gordes.

COPACABANA, Bolivia
The purple corn of Bolivia, Colombia, Ecuador and Peru makes for some remarkable-looking dishes and drinks, including the *api*, a hot smoothie-style sweet drink with hints of cinnamon, cloves, and citrus. Try it in Copacabana market on the shores of Lake Titicaca to to stave off the cold of the 3841m-high (12,601ft) high altiplano.

KITAKYUSHU, Japan
Away from Japan's cherry blossom mania, another often overlooked spring bloom is just as stunning, as this wisteria tunnel at the Kawachi Fujien Wisteria Garden in Kitakyushu shows. Late April to early May is the prime time to catch its numerous dome-shaped tunnels (up to 200m/656ft long) and swathes of wisteria rooftops.

KRUGER NATIONAL PARK, South Africa
This stern fellow, the lilac-breasted roller, is a Frankenstein-like mish mash when it comes to colours, boasting green, brown, blues, yellow, pink and lots of violet in its make-up. Look out for its rainbow hues on the branches of dead trees in grasslands and open woods throughout eastern and southern Africa, from Ethiopia and northwest Somalia to South Africa.

NAPLES, Italy
Away from its associations with Pompeii and ancient Rome, modern Naples is making art waves with its Metro Napoli Art Stations programme. This station, Toledo, by Oscar Tusquets Blanca, is themed around water and light. Catch equally arresting designs by the likes of Anish Kapoor, Gae Aulenti, Francesco Clemente and William Kentridge in some of the other stations.

MÉRIDA, Mexico
Elegant colonial architecture is just one reason to visit Yucatán's capital, Mérida. Another is its markets, in particular Mercado Municipal No 2 Santos Degollado and the iconic Mercado Lucas De Galvéz. Filled with stalls dedicated to local handicrafts, clothing and food products, they're great places to stock up on quirky buys like this traditional woven sombrero hat.

© MINNEAPOLIS PARKS AND RECREATION. COURTESY OF MEET MINNEAPOLIS

© TAEZO8 / GETTY IMAGES

© SL-PHOTOGRAPHY / SHUTTERSTOCK

PURPLE RAINDROP, USA

Unveiled in Minneapolis' Fairview Park in 2018, this 4.5m (15ft) tribute to the city's most famous son is coloured, of course, in a shade that's formally titled 'Purple Reign'. Part public art and part bench, it's the work of local sculptor Esther Osayande, and looks set to be a perfect selfie spot for those on a Prince pilgrimage to the home town of the original Purple One.

QUITO, Ecuador

It's Good Friday, and in Quito's Old Town, thousands of barefoot *cucuruchos* pour out of the church of San Francisco. In costumes symbolising humility and penitence, many of the men carry wooden crosses and flagellate themselves as they painfully walk the streets in the unique Procesión del Jesús del Gran Poder (Procession of Jesus the Almighty).

THE RED SEA, Egypt

Sporting venomous thorn-like spines resembling the biblical crown of thorns and with the ability to breathe through its feet, remove one of its two stomachs and replace lost limbs as necessary, the Crown of Thorns starfish is one of the largest starfish in the world — of more than 2000 known species in the world's oceans.

SOUTH ISLAND, New Zealand *(facing page)*

Along the shores of Lake Tekapo, the summer landscape bursts into colour as thousands of lupins paint the banks in swathes of purple, pink, yellow and blue. Catch them at their best here in late November, and around Lake Wanaka or along the riverbeds of Mackenzie Country, from mid-November to December.

BURSA, Turkey
Turkey is famous for its figs — it's the biggest producer in the world, with some 305,700 tonnes grown here annually. There's no better place than Bursa to seek out these succulent sweet treats: the local Black Bursa fig (coloured purple, despite the name) is said to be the primo variety. Head to the sprawling Kapalı Çarşı market to sample them dried or fresh from the tree.

PARIS, France
The stained glass of Sainte Chapelle, on the Île de la Cité in Paris's River Seine. The glasswork, featuring 1,113 scenes from the Bible on 15 13th-century windows soaring 15m (50ft) up to the vaulted ceiling, is a genuinely jaw-dropping sight, and yet is made up of just five colours; blue, red, yellow, green, and of course purple.

SHALATIN, Egypt *(facing page)*
Dried hibiscus flowers fill wooden containers on the east coast of Egypt, ready to be steeped and made into *karkad*, a sweet cold drink or hot tea similar to cranberry juice that's popular across Egypt and Sudan but also many other places across the globe; in the countries of the Caribbean it's known as sorrel, in West Africa, *bissap*.

JANITZIO ISLAND, Mexico
It's generally agreed that Janitzio Island in Michoacán's Patzcuaro lake is the place to celebrate Dia de Los Muertos or Day of the Dead, but you'll find these beautifully decorated sugar skulls and *papel picado* (pecked paper) tissue paper cut-outs throughout Mexico — often as *ofrendas* (offerings) on altars and headstones.

VERDE ISLANDS, Philippines
Thanks to its clear waters and impressive depths, the Verde Island Passage, a 16km-wide (10-mile) strait in the Phiippines's Batangas province, is one of the best diving spots in a region filled with very good diving spots. Among the nudibranchs, six-armed starfish, tigertail seahorses and dragonets, keep an eye out for this purple brain coral.

BRAEMAR, Scotland
This nimble-footed Highland dancer shows off his skills during the Braemar Royal Highland Gathering at the Princess Royal and Duke of Fife Memorial Park. Held annually on the first Saturday of September, its large number of competitions are matched only by the large numbers of tartans on display — drawn from an estimated 7000 different colourways and patterns.

GARDENS BY THE BAY, Singapore *(facing page)*
Brash and over-the-top or magical and memorising? The giant steel and concrete 'supertrees' of Singapore's Gardens by the Bay come ablaze in the Garden Rhapsody lightshow twice a night, illuminating a forest of real-world counterparts clustered far below them. Dine or drink in one of the trees, or get a bird's eye view of the spectacle from a suspended walkway.

LONDON, England
Sumptuous purple velvet and soft ermine make the 2.23kg (nearly 5lbs) weight of St Edward's Crown a little easier to bear by a new monarch at their coronation, which is the only time it's ever worn. The rest of the time, the solid gold crown set with semi-precious stones is the centrepiece of the Crown Jewels in the Tower of London.

ARTSCIENCE MUSEUM, Singapore

For a more natural colour show than the supertrees of Singapore's Gardens by the Bay, head to the ArtScience Museum on the Marina Bay Sands resort. The museum's lotus-flower 'hand', designed by renowned eco-conscious architect Moshie Safadie, is matched by a real lotus flower pond in front of it, fed by a waterfall of rainwater collected on the bowl-shaped roof of the building.

QUEENSLAND, Australia

Glistening with slime in its early life and arresting in both its size and purple hues, the cortinarius archeri is a member of the cortinarius genus, the largest genus of mushrooms in the world. Native to Australia, it puts in an appearance each autumn in eucalypt forests across Queensland, South Australia and Western Australia.

NEW YORK, USA

Competing manfully with the glittering lights of Manhattan across the East River, Domino Park in Brooklyn's South Williamsburg puts on its own light show for park-goers relaxing on the Pyramid of Seating Steps. It's a great spot from which to enjoy the 88 individually programmable water jets and lights of the super child-friendly fountain.

PANTANAL MATOGROSSENSE NATIONAL PARK, Brazil
A pair of hyacinth macaws perch together on a branch in the tropical wetland area of the Pantanal. It's not just their gorgeous plummage that makes them stand out; their size — from the tops of their heads to the tip of their long pointed tails, they're about 100cm (3.3ft) long — makes them longer than any other species of parrot.

ORURO, Bolivia
The biggest carnival in Bolivia is a frantic and colourful air, but purple is particularly prevalent across the costumes of the 400,000 people it attracts, and is a key colour of costumes worn by the Diabladas, the participants of the Diablada or Danza de los Diablos (Dance of the Devils).

NORTH MALE, Maldives
This magnificent sea anemone (Heteractis magnifica) on a coral reef in the Maldives makes a lovely sight, highlighting the smybiotic relationship of the lifeforms. The sea anemone hosts up to 12 species of anemonefish and is widespread in the Indo-Pacific, where you'll find it in coral and rocky reefs exposed to current and light.

KERALA, India

The lustrous purple skins of aubergines make them an alluring part of market stalls around the world, particularly the markets of India, where the berry (by botanical definition) was first grown domestically. In southern Indian states such as Kerala it is regarded as the king of vegetables; find it piled high at Cochin's Ernakulam Market, Asia's largest wholesale bazaar.

PROVENCE, France

Provence is awash with lavender-scented toiletries, but to glean engaging facts about the plant's history and its relationship with the region before filling your shopping basket, head to Le Musée de la Lavande in the drystone village of Cabrieres d'Avignon. In summer months, the museum offers demonstrations of distillation techniques using a traditional open-flame still.

BUENOS AIRES, Argentina

The startling contrast between near-black bark and pale indigo flowers make Jacaranda trees look lovely wherever they appear, but in Buenos Aires, where they form tunnels across wide boulevards, create soft floral carpets in parks and canopies in squares, and generally make the city sing with the arrival of spring, their presence is utterly magical.

DOURO, Portugal

The dusky purple hue of Tempranillo grapes along the Douro valley, where the vineyards stretch for more than 112km (70 miles) along the River Douro. Neat terraces rising up from the valley floor turn the landscape into beautiful stepped contours, and the train journey here, from Porto to Pocinho, is one of the world's great train rides.

PINK

© KATA716 / GETTY IMAGES

© ANDY-KIM MÜLLER / 500PX

© VACLAV SEBEK / SHUTTERSTOCK

FUJI, Japan

Each May, the fields south of Lake Motosuko in the Fuji Five Lakes area burst into impossibly vibrant hues of pink as the region's 800,000 stalks of *shibazakura* (pink moss, or phlox moss in English) fill the landscape as far as the eye can see. The Fuji Shibazakura festival, typically held from mid-April to early June, celebrates the spectacle.

SONORAN DESERT, USA

The USA's only venomous lizard, the gila monster, occasionally emerges from its underground burrows in the Sonoran, Mojave and Chihuahuan deserts on cool days. If you're lucky enough to see one, don't get too close; while it can only run up to about a mile an hour, if it latches onto you, it will not let go, chewing into your flesh to deposit its (non-lethal) venom.

TSODILO HILLS, Botswana

With 400 rock art sites containing more than 4000 paintings, it's no wonder the Tsodilo Hills region of northwest Botswana has been dubbed 'the Louvre of the desert'. As an added bonus, visit when the setting sun lights up the western cliffs with what locals call the 'Copper Bracelet of the Evening' for a magical experience.

KIMBA, Australia *(previous page)*

A female rose-breasted cockatoo, also known as a galah, distinguished by her pronounced pink eyes. These widely distributed parrots are found in open areas across all but the most arid parts of Australia, but if you don't spot one, Kimba, in South Australia, has a wooden one 7m (23ft) high outside the Halfway Across Australia Gem Shop on the Eyre Highway.

GUATIZA, Lanzarote
Local artist and architect César Manrique's beautiful Jardín de Cactus in the desolate black volcanic *malpaís* badlands of Lanzarote is a startling sight. With more than 1100 species of cacti, it's a great example of how his spatial interventions across the island sympathetically marry art and nature. The nearby plantations of prickly pears add to its special appeal.

PUTRAJAYA, Malaysia
The rosy-pink granite Masjid Putra (Putra mosque) has a captivatingly delicate design. With its ornate pink and white dome, it's a fine mix of graceful Middle Eastern and traditional Malay styles, and just one example of the extraordinary late-20th-century architecture to be found in the majestic city of Putrajaya.

YUCATÁN, Mexico
The aptly named Las Coloradas, a set of lagoons forming part of the Ria Lagartos Biosphere Reserve, range from yellow to this pretty pink, created by a high concentration of salt and microscopic algae. With their white salt borders, the effect is unforgettable, especially if you're lucky enough to see a flock of native flamingos rise up over the colourful dreamscape.

© ED REEVE

© ELLEON / GETTY IMAGES

© TRAVEL AND STILL LIFE PHOTOGRAPHY / GETTY IMAGES

LONDON, England
The ritzy Sketch tea room and bar in London's ritzy Mayfair is famed for its interior design. This space, the Gallery, designed by India Madhavi and featuring a number of colourful artworks by David Shrigley, is at the heart of the experience, its plushly pink bourgeois design creating a playful contrast with the artist's witty work, which features on the Gallery's tableware as well as its walls.

VARANASI, India
Getting its colour from the ochre covering the elaborate five segments of its exterior, the 18th-century Shri Durga Temple, aka the Monkey Temple (for the many monkeys that populate the site), is one of the most famous places of worship in the holy city of Varanasi. You'll find it in a walled enclosure 4km south of Godaulia.

EDUARDO AVAROA ANDEAN FAUNA RESERVE, Bolivia
In the southwest of Bolivia's altiplano, the vast Laguna Colorada, or coloured lagoon, startles with its pink-hued shallow water. It's all in the minerals, apparently, which also account for the equally remarkable emerald-green waters in the reserve's — yes, you guessed it — Laguna Verde. Chilean, Andean and endangered James flamingos add more pink tones.

© LOTTIE DAVIES / LONELY PLANET

KALAAT M'GOUNA, Morocco
Fragrant roses picked in the fields of the remote M'Goun Valley in the Atlas Mountains each spring. The end of harvest is celebrated with a huge rose festival (usually held in mid-May) in Kalaat M'Gouna. Expect serious partying and many, many rose-themed products and souvenirs to eat, drink, and take home.

SAMUT PRAKAN, Thailand
Inside, it's this pink domed roof with its elaborate stained-glass window that makes visitors to the Erawan Museum gasp. But that's as nought to what they'll have seen to get here; the museum's five storeys are contained within a huge bronze elephant-sculpture of Airavata, or Erawan, Indra's three-headed elephant mount from Hindu mythology.

ORANJESTAD, Aruba
With a colourful nod to its colonial past, the island of Aruba in the southern Caribbean contains a whimsical array of ornately decorated pastel Dutch Colonial Revival-style buildings in its downtown area. Once you've explored them, head to Fort Zoutman for the weekly Bon Bini festival to catch folk music, artisan goodies and Aruban cuisine.

© PIPAT KAMMA / SHUTTERSTOCK

© GOSS IMAGES / ALAMY STOCK PHOTO

CALPE, Spain

Ricardo Bofill loved colour. Here in Calpe, a southern Spanish town facing Algiers, the bright pink exterior of his postmodern apartment complex La Muralla Roja (the red wall) accentuates the contrast with the landscape and references Arab Mediterranean architecture, complete with the flat rooftops and interlocking stair of a typical casbah.

LAKE HILLIER, Australia *(facing page)*

Most bodies of water are coloured blue on maps, but if you were drawing the Recherche Archipelago's famous Lake Hillier, you'd need a pink crayon to accurately depict its striking colour. Standing in stark contrast to the deep blue waves of the Southern Ocean just metres away, its bubble-gum hue retains its pink colour even in a bottle.

HOKKAIDO, Japan

Each spring, the hillside Takinoue Park on Hokkaido bursts into an extensive carpet of pink as its millions of *shibazakura*, or pink moss phlox, bloom. There is, naturally, a festival celebrating the fact; the Takinoue Shibazakura Matsuri (meaning 'spring has sprung') festival begins in early May and runs for around a month until early June.

SHIRAZ, Iran

This rose-hued beauty, the Nasir al-Mulk or Pink Mosque, is one of southern Iran's most elegant examples of architecture. Built at the end of the 19th century, its interiors are particular stunning in the morning, when the light streaming through the stained-glass windows turns the hall and its Persian carpets into a kaleidoscope.

CAPE FLORISTIC, South Africa
Although you'll find the king protea on numerous South African symbols, including its coat of arms, the national cricket team's official crest and the Springboks' jerseys, the best place to see the country's national flower in all its natural glory is in its endemic home, the Cape Floristic Region, where the impressive artichoke-like blooms are abundant.

LAKE NAKURU NATIONAL PARK, Kenya
Time was when the millions — literally, estimates say up to two million — of pink flamingos feeding on the algea of Lake Nakuru were described by ornithologists as the greatest bird spectacle in the world. Their numbers have decreased over the years, but to see them take to the skies during their peak season of July and August is still a glorious sight.

KANSAI, Japan *(facing page)*
There are many, many options, but for numerous fans, western Japan's Kansai is *the* region in which to celebrate the country's national obsession, *sakura* (cherry blossom) season. From early March, visitors and locals flock to sites like Maruyama Park in Kyoto and Osaka Castle or Nishinomaru Garden in Osaka city to enjoy the sight of thousands of trees in bloom.

ANZA-BORREGO DESERT STATE PARK, USA
A rare burst of spring wildflowers in southern California's Anza-Borrego State Park. The park's more than 200 flowering plant species put on a brilliant display each spring, if winter rains have fallen at the right time. As flowering can take place any time between February and April, predicting their arrival is tough, but the hotline offers good information (+1 760-767-4684).

© BRASIL2 / GETTY IMAGES

© ZHWUN / SHUTTERSTOCK

© MUSTANG_79 / GETTY IMAGES

MANAUS, Brazil
Deep in Brazil's Amazon rainforest, looking for all the world like the kind of opera house Fitzcarraldo dreamed of in Werner Herzog's eponymous film, the Manaus Opera House, also known as the Amazon Theatre, is a vision of pale pink Renaissance grandeur. An annual opera festival is held here each April.

LESHAN, China
Moss-tinged but still regal, the 71m (233ft) giant Buddha of Leshan, hewn from the cliffs of Mount Emei near the Sichuan Province capital of Chengdu, is the largest stone-carved Buddha in the world. A winding staircase near its giant toenails leads to a viewing platform near its ear, a fine spot from which to take in its impressive scale.

CRETE, Greece
The pretty pink sands of Elafonissi beach, in southwestern Crete, regularly voted one of the world's best beaches. Pink crushed shells, broken coral pieces and calcium carbonate materials combine to create the colour, whose shades change depending on the motion of the tides.

© PHILIPPE LEJEANVRE | GETTY IMAGES

LESHAN, China

Still in Leshan, the beautiful ZhuoYing bridge (confusingly also known as the Haoshang bridge), is easy to miss despite being part of the complex containing the giant Buddha of Leshan (see opposite). To find it (and a lovely walk) take the Wuyou Temple route from the exit staircase of the giant Buddha.

WASHINGTON, DC, USA

Cherry trees in blossom along the banks of the Tidal Basin make a picture-perfect base for the Washington Monument. Each year, the National Cherry Blossom Festival takes place here from March to April, marking the 1912 gift of 3020 Japanese cherry trees from Tokyo to the city. Many more trees have been added since, creating a spectacular springtime sight.

HO CHI MINH CITY, Vietnam

The French colonial Tan Dinh church is one of Saigon's most loved buildings, and definitely its most pink. From its salmon-pink exterior, repainted in 1957, to exuberant bright pink columns and walls through the nave and sanctuary, it's a delight. The elaborately decorated Italian altar is the icing on the cake.

© SEANPAVONEPHOTO | GETTY IMAGES

© DASHA. ROMANOVA | GETTY IMAGES

© PAKIN SONGMOR / GETTY IMAGES

© SYLVAIN CORDIER / GETTY IMAGES

© PIXELSHOP / SHUTTERSTOCK

LARUNG GAR, Tibet
Tens of thousands of students, monks and nuns live and study in these red log cabins at Seda Larung Wuming Buddhist Institute, high up in China's remote Garze Tibetan Autonomous Prefecture. Founded in 1980, the institute is the largest and most influential centre for the study of Tibetan Buddhism in the world.

RIO NEGRO, Brazil
The Amazon river dolphin, or *boto*, a freshwater dolphin that inhabits the waterways of the Amazon and Orinoco in South America. This male – distinguished by his brighter pink colouring than a female – is playing in Brazil's Rio Negro, where inquisitive *botos* have been known to approach fishermen's canoes and make off with their paddles.

AIGUES-MORTES, France
Pink salt marshes are not uncommon around the world, but ones that are home to pink flamingos are harder to find; welcome then to Aigues-Mortes, in southern France. Famous for millennia for its high-quality salt, it's now equally famous for its long-legged residents – take the *petit train* to best take it all in.

KYOTO, Japan
Surely there are no sweets in the world more beautiful than Japan's *wagashi*? And in Japan, the most loved *wagashi* are the *nerikiri*. Made from sticky rice flour, sugar and white bean paste moulded into flowers, fruits and birds to represent the changing seasons, *nerikiri* are, like all *wagashi*, exquisitely crafted pops of colour whose function is as much about aesthetic as taste.

MAGDEBURG, Germany
Named for its lush grass roof, the Grüne Zitadelle (Green Citadel) in the central German city of Magdeburg is, according to its creator, Friedensreich Hundertwasser, an 'oasis for humanity and nature in a sea of rational houses'. This oasis literally is a living thing, its undulating walls dotted with plant life and its colour a smile-inducing constant in the city.

PETRA, Jordan
The rose-red city of Petra, so-called for the colour of the rock from which much of the prehistoric site was carved, has been wowing humans on and off (off being when it disappeared for a good millennia until its rediscovery in the 19th century) for at least 2000 years, and despite its popularity, it will wow you too. Trust us.

© BYELIKOVA_OKSANA / GETTY IMAGES

JAIPUR, India

Giving Petra (p105) a run for its money as the pink city, Jaipur exudes pink from its very pores, from the ochre-pink defensive walls and city gates to the buildings along its bustling streets. And the 1799 Hawa Mahal palace, with its multiple balconies and ornamental windows, is a serious contender for the world's most winning pink building.

HIMEJI CITY, Japan

For many *sakura* fans, the place to head during blossom time is Himeji City. Here the startling white Himeji Castle and the sharp lines of the modern city contrast with thousands of cherry blossom trees in bloom to create a pink-and-white marriage made in cherry-blossom heaven. It's an easy bullet-train ride of an hour from Osaka or Kyoto.

UDON THANI, Thailand *(facing page)*

You'll see pictures of Nong Han Lake, aka the Red Lotus Sea, all over Udon, but getting to see the real thing can take some work. Time your visit for early December to February, head 40km (24 miles) southeast of Udon city to Ban Dieam, hire a boat early in the morning (the flowers close by 10.30am) and head into the heart of the lake to see a magical carpet woven from thousands of tropical pink water lilies.

PUGET SOUND, USA

Named for their resemblance to Dickensian quill ink pens, bright pink sea pens, a type of soft coral, are hardy sorts, living up to a ripe old 100. They glow in the dark, and while generally living at great depths or on the ocean floor, at Washington state's Puget Sound they can sometimes be seen on low-tide days in the water's soft sediments.

© JIH-CHI CHAN / GETTY IMAGES

© JODI JACOBSON / GETTY IMAGES

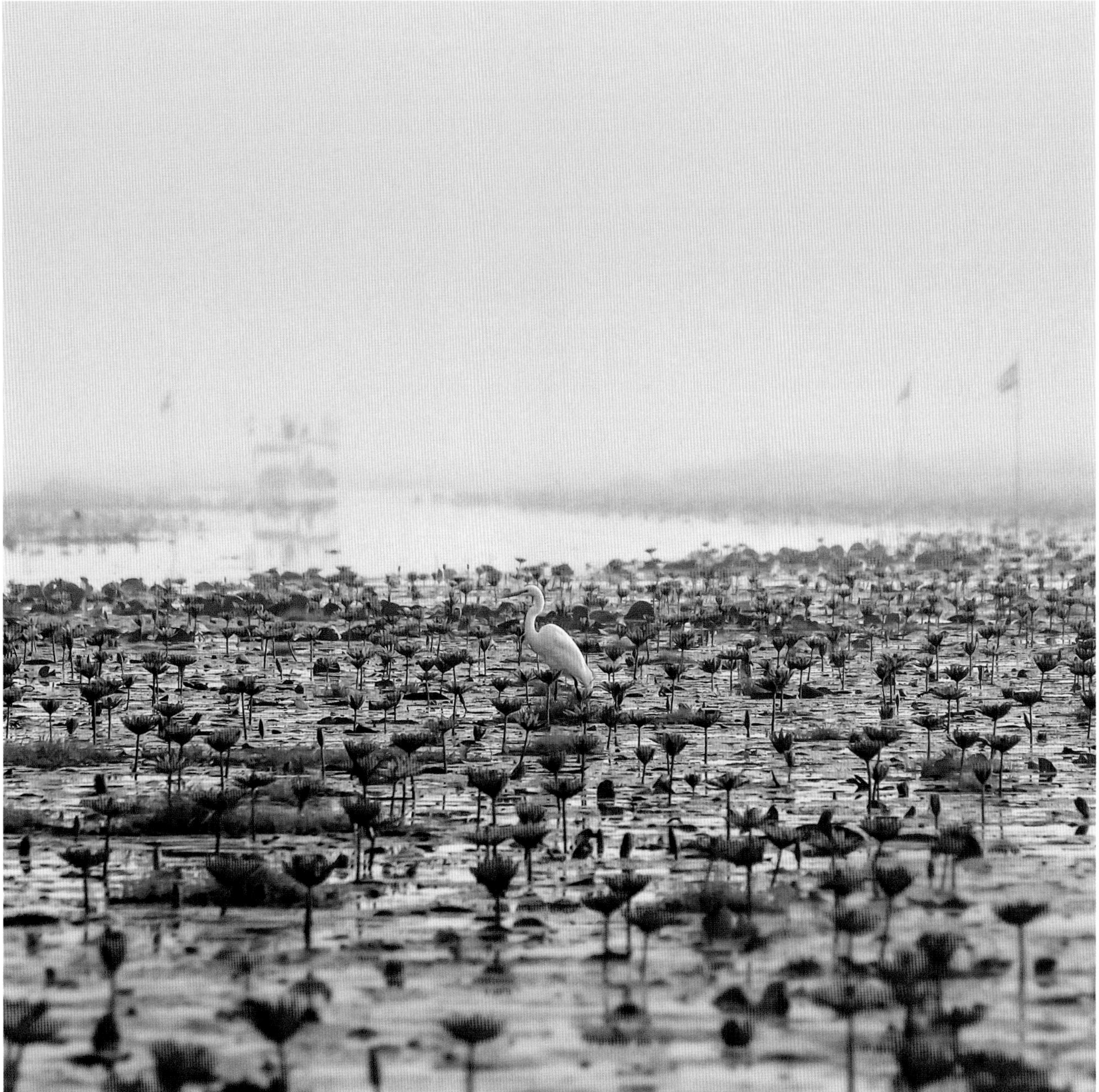

KALEIDOSCOPE

BANGKOK, Thailand
Like markets? You'll love Bangkok's Chatuchak (aka JJ Market), which, with more than 15,000 stalls across 26 sections (among them pets, vintage, homeware, produce and plants), lays claim to being the world's largest weekend market. Now in its fifth iteration and fourth location, the market can be bewildering to navigate; use the clock tower as a landmark.

BARCELONA, Spain
The bright mosaics of Antoni Gaudí's Park Guell shimmer in Catalonian sunshine, lending an enchanting air to the natural-world motifs decorating its central area, walkways and fountains. Wandering along the covered paths, taking in Gaudí's twisted stonework columns and sinuous shapes, is a real treat – as is a rest on the famous curving tiled bench designed by architect Josep Maria Jujol.

TENNESSEE, USA
Since its inaugural 1970 protest march marking New York's Stonewall Riots of 1969, Pride has spread from Sydney and Tel Aviv to Miami and Manchester in the UK, which has held a parade since 1985. In 2019, another Manchester got in on the act: Manchester, Tennessee was the site for this Pride march, which took place as part of the Bonnaroo Music And Arts Festival.

ANDASIBE–MANTADIA NP, Madagascar
(previous page)
Some of the world's most colourful lizards are native to Madagascar — among them the minor's chameleon and panther chameleon. The male panther chameleon can grown to around 45cm (17in) in length, so you've a fair chance of seeing one, particularly during the rainy season of October to March, when mating males become even more vividly coloured.

BUSAN, South Korea
Every year in the fortnight leading up to Buddha's birthday in May, temples in South Korea light up in dazzling displays. Busan's Samgwangsa Temple offers one of the biggest and best, with an intricate geometric arrangement composed of thousands of lanterns. Climb the hill to the shrine of Jijang-jeon to see the lights come on and get a bird's-eye view of this brilliant event.

TAICHUNG, Taiwan
The eye-poppingly colourful village of Tainchung is more hamlet than village, but with every inch of it covered in bright motifs, it's a must-see attraction. It's all the work of one man, former soldier Huang Yung-Fu, who began painting what was meant to be temporary post-war army housing in a bid to stave off its threatened demolition. It worked — the site is now preserved.

RIO DE JANEIRO, Brazil
It might look like a melange of mayhem and madness, but as with most carnivals, Rio's is a well-ordered parade, with 'schools' or 'bands' of revellers using dance and costumes to interpret narratives that often take in history and culture as well as music. For its 300th anniversary, expect 2023's daily attendance to far surpass the usual two million. Book your spot now.

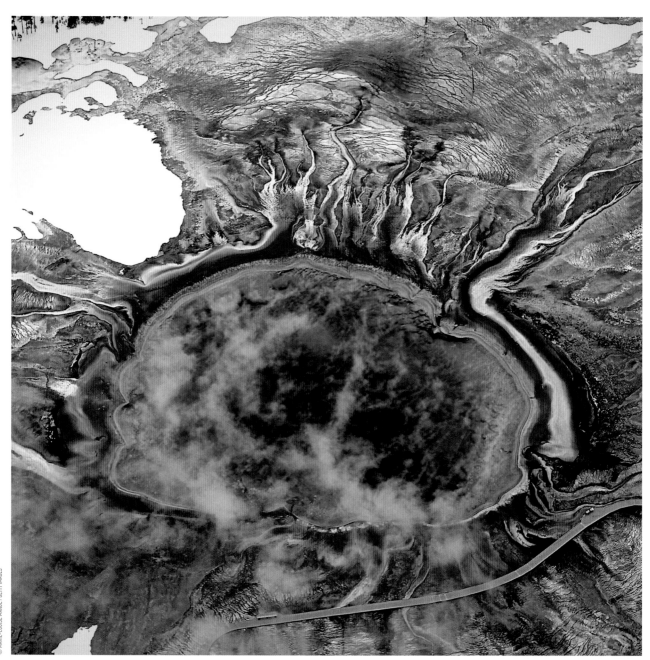

© MING TANG-EVANS / LONELY PLANET

PARIS, France
Does any biscuit look as elegantly appealing as a macaron? Pierre Hermé, master patissier and baker of arguably the best in the world, would almost certainly say *non*. He began to introduce flavours such as pistachio, quince and fig, combining them with spices, citrus and floral notes, in the 1980s, and his colourful collections are now the acme of sophisticated sweet biscuits.

GUATAPÉ, Colombia
Gaily painted *chiva* buses are common in rural Colombia, where they transport people, livestock and livelihoods across the country. Outside, colours usually incorporate the yellow, blue, and red of the flags of Ecuador and Colombia, while inside, bench seats and a mix of metal and wood combine to create an object of cultural curiosity and pride to both their drivers and passengers.

YELLOWSTONE NP, USA *(facing page)*
The Grand Prismatic Spring is the largest of Yellowstone's impressive range of hot springs — and, with its malevolent eyeball looking like an entry to Hades, surely its most striking. Set in the Midway Geyser Basin, the colours are created by bacteria formed in the varying temperatures of the spring, which reach as much as 87°C (189°F) in the centre, where the hot spring waters emerge.

HARBIN, China
You might expect the Harbin International Ice and Snow Sculpture Festival, held each January, to be defined by blinding white creations (see p143), but in the Ice and Snow World arena bright multicoloured lights illuminate extensive structures made using huge blocks of ice from the nearby Songhua River. Tempted? Bring warm clothes; winter lows of –35°C (–31°F) are not uncommon.

© CHRIS MOUYIARIS / ROBERT HARDING

© GAVIN HELLIER / AWL IMAGES

SANTIAGO SACATEPÉQUEZ, Guatemala

Gigantic bright kites dipping and diving over a cemetery? It can only be Central America on the Day of the Dead — specifically, Santiago Sacatepéquez in Guatemala. The townsfolk here spend weeks crafting cloth, paper and bamboo kites, before taking them to the cemetery to honour their departed with food, flowers and kite displays, believed to be a form of communication with the dead.

KAUAI, Hawaii

The bark of a rainbow eucalyptus tree features a startling array of bright tones, including lavender, blue, green, orange and maroon, as it goes through different phases of its shedding and renewal cycle. The multi-coloured tree has been a feature of Hawaii since 1929, when it was introduced on Oahu as part of a reforestation programme. A great place to see it these days is at the Keahua Arboretum in Wailua, on Kauai's east coast.

MATHURA, India

The sheer exuberance of Holi, the Hindu festival celebrating spring and love, is beautifully expressed with literally tonnes of colour each year throughout India (see p40), Nepal and, increasingly, parts of Southeast Asia too. If you want to take part, be prepared to be covered head to toe with coloured paint, be it in powder or liquid form — the latter usually delivered via water guns and balloons.

MYLAPORE, India

Tamil Nadu is famed for temples featuring elaborate *gopura* (gateway towers) that soar into the sky like so many surreal, gaudy funfair attractions, adorned with scenes from Hindu texts. Kapaleeswarar temple near Chennai is one of the most famous, its 40m (130ft) tall *gopuram* decorated with an impressive menagerie of animal statues. Nearby, Madurai's Meenakshi Temple goes 13 better with its 14 colourful *gopura*.

LITTLE INDIA, Singapore

Once the preserve of rich Europeans taking a flutter on the horses at its racecourse, Singapore's Little India is, as the name suggests, a taste of India – in super-Technicolor. Indian restaurants, temples and shops fill the streets with colour, while street-food vendors and *chai wallahs* fill them with the smells and tastes of the country.

BURANO, Italy

Set on Venice's lagoon, the archipelago of Burano is filled with hundreds of little houses in strictly government-regulated colours that create an astonishing palette of vibrant tones. Linked by bridges and criss-crossed with canals that reflect the rainbow colours of the houses, approaching across the water and exploring the bright alleyways of the four islands is an unforgettable experience.

HOI AN, Vietnam

The former port town of Hoi An in central Vietnam is illuminated nightly with thousands of colourful lanterns shimmering in the waters of its many canals. The lanterns add a magical note to an appealing city that's filled with architecture spanning ancient wooden shop-houses and merchant houses, temples, French colonial buildings and ornate Vietnamese tube houses.

RIO DE JANEIRO, Brazil

The 250 steps of Escadaria Selarón were a true labour of love for their creator, the Chilean-born painter and sculptor Jorge Selarón. The thousands of tiles, ceramic fragments and broken mirrors decorating the steps were collected from over 60 countries around the world, gifted to the artist by fans or painted by Selarón himself, who lived in a house next to the steps until his death in 2013.

MANAROLA, Italy

Precariously perched along some of the most dramatic coastline in the world and connected only by boat, a 19th-century railway line and miles of sinuous footpaths and mountain trails, the five medieval fishing village of Cinque Terre, including this one, Manarola, offer a rainbow spectrum of terraced houses, vines and gardens tumbling down the cliffs.

LISSE, The Netherlands
As the world's main producer of tulips, large swathes of the Netherlands are painted in broad stripes of vivid colour each spring, particularly in the Bollenstreek region, where from March to May some three billion of the flowers are grown. Seven million bulbs are planted in the 32ha (80 acre) Keukenhof Park, which is almost as impressive, with landscaped gardens and greenhouses.

VINICUNCA, Peru
More than 5000m (16,500ft) high up in the Andes, the Vinicunca, or Montaña de Siete Colores, stuns visitors with its seven bands of colour created by different minerals in the peak, and seen at their best in the dry season. Another rainbow peak – the Cerro de los Siete Colores – lies across the border in Argentina's Purmamarca.

MEXICO CITY, Mexico
Despite their Mexican motifs and decoration, the exuberant *lucha libre* masks worn by Mexican wrestlers are not an ancient part of the sport, but an American import of the 20th century. Still, Mexican *enmascarados* have taken to them with gusto at the huge Arena Mexico in Colonia Doctores, the older Arena Coliseo in Colonia Cuauhtemoc, and the more intimate Arena Naucalpan.

© SUSANNE KREMER / 4CORNERS

TOKYO, Japan

With a chequered history that takes in swamp, duck sanctuary, purification plant and the planned but unrealised kabuki theatre which gives it its name, Tokyo's modern Kabukicho entertainment district houses restaurants, nightclubs, love hotels, massage parlours and hostess clubs along with literally thousands of bars and, of course, *pachinko* (slot-machine) parlours.

KUALA LUMPUR, Malaysia

Most people visiting the historic Hindu shrines and limestone caves that make up the Batu Caves have no idea that they'll have to climb these 272 colourful steps to get to them. The steps, colour-blocked since 2018, have an undeniable impact, and the army of macaque monkeys that terrorise tourists and pilgrims certainly haven't been daunted by their hues.

CAPE TOWN, South Africa *(facing page)*

Rows of brightly painted low-roofed houses make Cape Town's Bo-Kaap one of the most-photographed areas of the city. Initially an 18th-century garrison, freed slaves started to settle the area after emancipation in the 1830s, adding the bright colours to the facades of the house after apartheid. Two stand-out sites are the Bo-Kaap Museum and the Auwal Mosque, South Africa's oldest.

RAJA AMPAT, Indonesia

West Papua's Raja Ampat is truly paradisiacal, with some 1500 tiny islands set in some of the world's most abundant waters. Here are wobbegong, black-tip reef and walking epaulette sharks, sea snakes, giant gorgonians, blue and yellow fusiliers, angelfish, turtles, beautiful coral… Tempted? You'll need a minimum of 50 logged dives to see them and hundreds of other fish species.

© GODOLGLA / GETTY IMAGES

© IFISH / GETTY IMAGES

GOLD

© FARAWAY PHOTOS / ALAMY STOCK PHOTO

© MATT MUNRO / LONELY PLANET

© ANTONOVVITALII / SHUTTERSTOCK

VIENNA, Austria

The 2500 gilded iron laurel leaves cladding the cupola atop Joseph Maria Olbrich's art-nouveau Secession Building give it a regal bearing that's somewhat undermined by its local moniker, the 'golden cabbage'. Inside, Gustav Klimt's famous Beethoven Frieze uses more gold and other signature colours to create an arresting artwork featuring monsters and goddesses.

NIZHNY NOVGOROD, Russia

The striking white stone, green roof and golden domes of the Church of St John the Baptist make it a major attraction in Nizhny Novgorod. In a city famous for its places of worship, it's one of the oldest Orthodox churches, though centuries of rebuilding and transformation have altered its appearance radically since its 15th-century origins.

NYAUNG U, Myanmar

The archetypal stupa of Myanmar is gloriously illustrated in the golden Shwezigon Pagoda (or Shwezigon Paya), the Buddhist temple located in Nyaung U. With its five terraces topped by a central gold-leaf gilded cone it looks spectacular seen from afar. Close-up, Bagan's largest surviving bronze Buddhas are just some of the things that make a visit here so memorable.

AMRITSAR, India *(previous page)*

Amritsar's Golden Temple, locally known as the Harmandir Sahib or Darbar Sahib, rises ethereally from the holy lake it sits in, offering its hundreds of thousands of pilgrims the sight of a marble and copper temple whose upper half is encased in intricately engraved gold panels, topped by a gilded gold dome added in the 19th century.

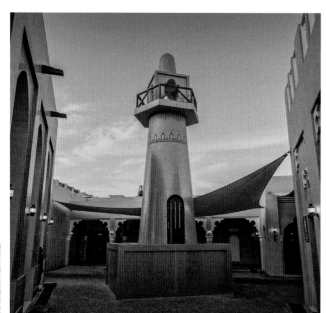

DOHA, Qatar
The purpose-built 'cultural village' of Katara is notable for a number of unusual sites, including the gorgeous Katara Masjid, striking brick and clay pigeon towers and a 5000-seater amphitheatre built in 2010 but resembling an ancient Greco-Roman space with Arab notes. But pride of place has to go to its Golden Masjid, covered in thousands of shimmering tiles.

GIZA, Egypt
The approximately 3350-year-old golden mask of King Tutankhamun, discovered by Howard Carter in 1925 in the Valley of the Kings. It was due to move from Cairo's Egyptian Museum to Giza's new Grand Egyptian Museum in 2020. Made of solid high-carat gold and inlaid with gems and stones including lapis lazuli, quartz and turquoise, it is one of the most famous artworks in the world.

KYOTO, Japan
The gold exterior of the Kinkaku-ji (Golden Pavilion) Zen temple, with gold-leaf covering its upper floors, is here ethereally reflected in its surrounding pool. Set alight a number of times in its centuries-old existence, the last time by a fanatic monk in 1950, the current iteration of the 14th-century original features different architectural styles on each floor and a golden phoenix.

© CULTURA / GETTY IMAGES

MYSORE, India
It apparently takes 98,260 light bulbs to achieve this glittering state for Karnataka's Mysore Palace, which has been illuminated every night for more than a century, with the help of four electrical substations whose efforts are synchronised via a red light on top of the palace's central dome. Inside, don't miss the Golden Throne or *howdah*, covered in 80kg (176lb) of intricately carved gold.

JAIPUR, India
Jaipur's City Palace is filled with jewel-like decorative elements, particularly in the Pritam Niwas Chowk courtyard — or 'courtyard of the beloved'. Here four elaborately decorated gates representing the four seasons include this standout one, the Northeast Peacock Gate, dedicated Lord Vishnu; look above the lintel of the door to see a small idol of the Hindu god.

DANANG, Vietnam *(facing page)*
Ancient meets modern in this golden bridge held aloft by two giant hands. Or does it? In fact the whole thing was dreamed up in 2018 for the Sun World Ba Na Hills entertainment complex in Danang, where the 150m (490ft) long pedestrian bridge connects with a cable car and a kitsch replica French village, gardens and amusement park.

KYAIKTIYO, Myanmar
The Kyaiktiyo or Golden Rock Pagoda may not literally be balanced on a strand of the Buddha's hair, as its thousands of daily pilgrims might believe, but with a tiny area of contact between the rock and underlying ground, it still looks precarious enough to marvel at how the granite boulder can have been so completely covered in gold leaf. Arrive at sunrise or sunset for the best views.

© MATT MUNRO / LONELY PLANET

© IMAGEBROKER / ALAMY STOCK PHOTO

© STEFANO RAVERA / ALAMY STOCK PHOTO

© ANTHONY WRIGHT / GETTY IMAGES

© KWANCHAI KHAMMUEAN / ALAMY STOCK PHOTO

LONDON, England
Fans of the gentle BBC comedy series *The Detectorists*, or anyone who's ever held a metal detector, will surely feel a tiny thrill on viewing the Fishpool Hoard. Housed at the British Museum, the find's 1237 15th-century gold coins, rings and other pieces of jewellery were discovered by workmen on a building site near present-day Cambourne Gardens in Ravenshead, Nottinghamshire.

VIENTIANE, Laos
The elegant, elongated lotus-bud shape of the three-tiered, 45m (148ft) high stupa of the Wat Pha That Luang is famous throughout Laos, and is believed to enshrine a breast bone of the Buddha brought here as early as the 3rd century BC by Ashokan missionaries from India. Lao and Khmer sculptures are set around the stupa.

PARIS, France
At 4m (13ft), she's not particularly tall, but Emmanuel Frémiet's 1874 gilded bronze statue *Jeanne d'Arc* dominates the 1st arrondissement's Place des Pyramides, near the site where the fearless warrior was wounded trying to take Paris in 1429. She was modelled by Aimée Girod, fittingly born in Domrémy, the same Lorraine village as Jeanne.

ABU DHABI, UAE

Shiny, expensive and more than a kilometre long, the Emirates Palace hotel in Abu Dhabi may not be somewhere you can afford or want to stay, but a visit is a must. You can usually wander around freely, but to learn more about the hotel's numerous gold-leaf ceilings, adorned with 22-carat gold imported from Italy, a guided tour is an illuminating experience.

DUBAI, UAE

Even if you're not in the market for the world's largest gold ring (the Star of Taiba, on display in the market), wander through Dubai's gold souk for a seriously blinging eye-assault courtesy of the 400-odd gold, diamond and silver retailers working from a space which has been in place here for almost a century.

STOCKHOLM, Sweden

The magnificent Gyllene Salen or Golden Hall in Stockholm's City Hall is impressive in both decor and size, its 44m (144ft) length making it perfect for the ball held here after the Nobel Prize dinner. Its originally granite and stone walls were decorated with their gold mosaic tiles — 18 million of them — following a generous private donation in the early 20th century.

VERSAILLES, France

With its 100,000 gold leaves crafted into different emblems associated with the French monarchy, the golden gate of Versailles is a magnificent beast, but it's not the original. Not that you'd know: in 2008, a bevy of historians, gilders and ironsmiths were brought in to ensure this is an exact replica of Jules Hardouin-Mansart's 17th-century original.

VIANA DO CASTELO, Portugal

A local woman shows off her *chieira* (a regional term for vanity or pride) in the Mordomia Parade. Held each August, the women-only event sees hundreds of participants in colourful traditional costumes or more sombre black wedding dresses don as much as 7kg (15lbs) of real gold to parade through the streets.

BALLARAT, Australia

Australia's great 1850s gold rushes are enjoyably recreated and explored at Sovereign Hill, and we're not just saying that... it's been named Australia's best 'Major Tourist Attraction' four times. Along with mines and a gold museum, there's a chance to try your hand at panning; you're not likely to get anything like this haul, but if you do find anything, it's yours to keep.

BANGKOK, Thailand

The reclining Buddha of Wat Pho, resplendent in the gold leaf that covers its magnificent 46m (151ft) long body. As one of Bangkok's oldest temples it's a must for visitors, who try to make wishes come true by dropping coins into the 108 bronze bowls lined up at the base of the walls. The complex's other 394 gilded Buddha statues from different parts of Thailand sit beatifically in the lotus position.

ST PETERSBURG, Russia

The Winter Palace and State Hermitage Museum (see p62) are filled with grand interiors, among them the ceremonial Armorial Hall shown here. The fluted columns are just one part of its magnificent interior by Vasily Stasov; what he would have made of its post-revolution use as a concert hall for the masses is anyone's guess.

SOFIA, Bulgaria

The 19th-century Orthodox St Alexander Nevsky Cathedral may be dwarfed by the growing number of high-rises in Bulgaria's capital, but its 45m (148ft) gilded gold dome and 53m (174ft) bell tower ensure it stands out from the crowd. One of the largest Christian church buildings in the world, it's able to accommodate up to 10,000 people.

AUROVILLE, India

This startling edifice, the Matrimandir or Temple of the Mother, lies at the heart of an experimental township devoted to unity, but can be enjoyed by all from a viewing point in a tranquil garden. Clad in 1414 steel discs covered in gold leaf and symbolising the birth of a new consciousness, it houses a pure crystal-glass globe lit by sunlight in an opening at the apex of the sphere.

INNSBRUCK, Austria

The late-Gothic bay roof and loggia known as the Goldenes Dachl (Golden Roof) shine out in the city of Innsbruck, thanks to the 2657 fire-gilded copper tiles covering the open balcony. You can see a picture of the man who commissioned it, Emperor Maximilian I, in sculpted reliefs on the balcony balustrade, though the 16th-century originals reside in the Tyrolean State Museum.

VIENNA, Austria *(facing page)*

Edmund Hellmer's gold-plated statue of Johann Strauss shines bright on a winter's day in Vienna's famous Stadtpark — home also to sculptures of fellow composers Johannes Brahms, Franz Schubert and Franz Léhar. Should the presence of so many musicians inspire you to listen to some, the Kursalon concert venue sits opposite the statue.

BIRMINGHAM, England

Locally known as the Golden Boys (or more wittily by Brummie wags, the Carpet Salesmen), this gilded bronze statue by William Bloye and Raymond Forbes-Kings honouring Matthew Boulton, James Watt, and William Murdoch shows the Industrial Revolution pioneers studying steam engine plans. Not carpets. Removed in rebuilding works, they're due back in town in September 2020.

SILVER

HELSINKI, Finland

If one thing encapsulates a city that feels both ancient and modern, spiritual and functional, man-made and natural, it's surely Eila Hiltunen's 1967 monument to the composer Jean Sibelius. The abstract piece of more than 600 hollow steel organ pipes representing the spirit of Sibelius' music was disliked by many, hence the large figurative representation of Sibelius in the foreground.

TULAMBEN, Bali

A school of black jacks swarms around the wreck of the USS Liberty. The ship has been submerged here for more than 50 years, when it was pushed off the beach it had limped onto in 1942 after being torpedoed by a Japanese submarine. It's now covered in healthy coral growth, with a plethora of soft corals and large and small fish species.

GRUYÈRES, Switzerland

This otherworldly bar will be immediately familiar to fans of the *Alien* movies, who will find it, and the rest of the Giger Museum it's housed in, irresistible. HR Giger was the surrealist artist who conceived of the terrifying xenomorph back in the 1970s, and in his medieval hilltop chateau, the mix of film design, erotic art, personal art collection and this bar make an arresting — if unsettling — excursion.

FALKIRK, Scotland *(previous page)*

These impressive beasts, clad in 990 stainless steel panels each, stand more than 30m (100ft) tall in the Helix, a parkland project near Falkirk. Created by equine sculptor Andy Scott, the Kelpies were modelled on two real-life Clydesdale horses, Duke and Baron, to honour the historic importance of the horse to Scotland's economy.

BRUSSELS, Belgium

Post-war Europe's optimistic belief in an atomic-age future led by science and learning is nicely illustrated in this striking structure, the Atomium, constructed for the 1958 Brussels World Expo. Representing a unit cell of an iron crystal, magnified 165 billion times, its nine connected stainless steel-clad spheres (originally covered in aluminium) include a restaurant with extensive views.

PARIS, France

In designing the Philharmonie de Paris concert hall, architect Jean Nouvel returned to his love of metal to create this low-slung stunner which he says is harmonised with four elements of the city. His relationship with the client was less harmonious; unhappy with the 'non-compliance' with his original design, he applied for a court order to disassociate himself from the project.

LUANG PRABANG, Laos

In Laos' Luang Prabang province, the quality and workmanship of traditional Hmong silver jewellery inspires hundreds of modern-day silversmiths to create their own versions of the tribal rings, bracelets and neck rings worn by the hill tribe for centuries. Find hundreds of sellers at the laid-back Luang Prabang Night Market, where some 300 Hmong and Lao vendors ply their trade.

© NINO MARCUTTI / ALAMY STOCK PHOTO

© SAMANTHAINALADIHLSEN / SHUTTERSTOCK

© TRAVEL PIX COLLECTION / AWL IMAGES LTD

MOSCOW, Russia

This beautiful view of the 107m (351ft) titanium rocket of the Monument to the Conquerors of Space, impressively set at an angle of 77°, its exhaust plume trailing behind it, is a highlight of any trip to Moscow. Constructed in 1964 to celebrate the USSR's space exploration — in particular Yuri Gagarin's 1961 orbit of Earth — its modernist form is as striking now as it was then.

LOS ANGELES, USA

A stainless steel California Zephyr train from the 1940s, displayed at Union Station in 2018. Edward Budd's introduction of a corrugated stainless-steel exterior in the 1940s was such a hit that riding it from Chicago to San Francisco, its streamlined form snaking across the prairies of Nebraska and chugging through the heart of the Rockies, remains a popular experience for those with 53 hours to spare.

BILBAO, Spain *(facing page)*

If ever a building could have been said to have completely revitalised a city, Frank Gehry's Guggenheim Museum is surely it. Nowadays its undulating futuristic form is the norm, but in 1997, when it was opened, the titanium and glass building was hailed as an unqualified success by everyone — a rare thing in architecture. And, equally rarely, it was completed on time and on budget.

PARIS, France

When the beautiful Institut du Monde Arabe was inaugurated in 1987 as symbol of dialogue between Western culture and the Arab world, its elegant traditional Arab motifs set it apart from so many other metal heavy-facades. This aluminium structure is clever, too: 120 window apertures linked to photoelectric cells react to light levels to allow for natural light control based on the amount of sunshine.

© JOSE A. BERNAT BACETE / GETTY IMAGES

© UNIVERSALIMAGESGROUP / GETTY IMAGES

© ANDREW MONTGOMERY / LONELY PLANET

PARIS, France

A player waits to take his turn in pétanque, a game so popular in France that almost every park, square and scrubby bit of land contains a hard dirt or gravel court. The balls are generally chrome-plated steel, and, with 20 different steels and forms of tempering used by different manufacturers to claim attributes like corrosion resistance and impact strength, their selection can be bewildering.

BEIJING, China

The 2008 Summer Olympic Games were an opportunity for China to show the world how far it had come architecturally. And its National Stadium showed it was a long way indeed. Constructed of 110,000 tonnes (121,000 tons) of steel combined with a design of interlocking parts, its resemblance to woven twigs immediately resulted in its nickname of the Bird's Nest.

TBILISI, Georgia

Revered by Georgians as the Mother of Georgia, the aluminium *Kartlis Deda* statue by Tbilisi sculptor Elguja Amashukeli looms high on the top of Sololaki Hill, where she's been standing guard over the city since Tbilisi's 1500th anniversary in 1958. Depicted in Georgian national dress, she holds a bowl in one hand for friends, and a sword in the other for enemies.

CHIANG MAI, Thailand

The glittering silver, mirrors and bright colours that decorate the interior of the Wat Sri Suphan's *ubosot* (ordination hall), aptly also known as the Silver Temple, are only bested by the elaborate hand-crafted decoration exhibited on its exterior, where every inch is covered in silver. If it inspires you to take some home, the area's many silversmiths happily take on commissions.

NEW YORK, USA

For a short time after its construction in 1930, the Chrysler Building, with its distinctive art-deco tower, was the tallest building in the world. Almost a century on, it remains the tallest brick building in the world, and not a single sheet of the diamond-honed Enduro KA-2 steel cladding in its tower and spire has ever needed to be replaced.

CHICAGO, USA

Anish Kapoor's curvaceous, stainless-steel *Cloud Gate* sculpture was inspired by liquid mercury, and its seamless surface reflects and distorts the Chicago skyline. Set in the AT&T Plaza, and commonly known as 'the Bean', it's proved hugely popular with locals and visitors, but don't feel you have to rush to see it — Kapoor promised the city that it should survive for a thousand years.

WHITE

© MICHAEL WILSON / GETTY IMAGES

© BORCHEE / GETTY IMAGES

© JASON LANGLEY / ROBERT HARDING

WINDSOR, England

Time was when you could eat these elegant mute swans — as long as you were a swan-owning English aristocrat. Nowadays, the only indignity these elegant avians need endure is swan-upping, the annual counting ceremony held on the Thames between Sunbury and Abingdon each July. The tradition dates back to the 12th century, when the crown claimed ownership of all mute swans.

PARIS, France

The beautiful Sacré-Cœur basilica, designed by Paul Abadie and completed in 1914 with the help of six additional architects, stands tall and regal over the hills of Montmartre. Eschewing Paris's more gothic style for an airy, elegant Romano-Byzantine affair, the white travertine stone ensures its status as the city's most loved beacon.

SARAKINIKO, Greece

Rising up from the sea like gently sculpted vanilla ice cream, the startling white and grey-white rocks of Sarakiniko beach found on the north shore of the island of Milos are one of the most photographed landscapes in the Aegean. Carved out over millennia by wind and sea, the arresting volcanic rockscape is unique to the island.

ABU DHABI, UAE *(previous page)*

Abu Dhabi's Sheik Zayed Mosque is the UAE's largest mosque, but what makes it special is a determinedly global and inclusive outlook, with input from British, Italian and Emirati architects, design inspiration from Turkey, Morocco, Pakistan and Egypt, and an open-door policy which enables non-Muslims to experience its onion-top domes, reflective pools and vast prayer hall.

© CHRISTIAN KOBER / ROBERT HARDING

HARBIN, China

The world's largest ice and snow festival, held each year in Harbin, Heilongjiang, is rarely this white. Increasingly, sculptors using saws to carve ice taken from the frozen surface of the Songhua River employ multi-coloured lights (see p113) to make their huge ice-block attractions stand out from the crowd — and what a crowd; the 2017 festival attracted 18 million visitors.

UFFINGTON, England

The best-known of Britain's prehistoric hill figures, Oxfordshire's 110m (361ft) long Uffington White Horse is a real beauty, a chalk wonder some 3000 years old. The Bronze Age figure is not the only attraction here; Dragon's Hill, the Giant's Steps and the Manger add to the area's ancient appeal.

WHITE DESERT, Egypt

The surreal outcrops of Farafra are a rare sight in this part of the world, where sphinxes and pyramids are the big draws. The national park's massive chalk rock formations should be up there with them; that they're not, meaning very few other visitors, makes a trip here feel like a personal discovery.

© GARY CHALKER / GETTY IMAGES

© SEPPFRIEDHUBER / GETTY IMAGES

© GABRIELAER / GETTY IMAGES

LISBON, Portugal

Look for 30 of Portugal's heroes in this huge slab of concrete, among them Vasco da Gama, Ferdinand Magellan and King Manuel I. Set near the Tagus river in Lisbon and carved in the shape of the prow of a Portuguese caravel sailing ship, it's a tribute to Portugal's golden age of exploration in the 15th and 16th centuries.

WEST COAST, USA

The sweetly named pearly everlasting anaphalis numbers a respectable 110 species, but only one is native to North America; the western pearly everlasting (Anaphalis margaritacea), used by Native Americans for a range of medicinal purposes. To see them at their best, and most profuse, head for any of the West Coast's Golden Gate national parks from June to September.

YELLOWSTONE NP, USA *(facing page)*

Yellowstone National Park is one of the world's top geothermal splendours. Features such as fumaroles, geysers, hot springs, mudpots and travertine terraces make a visit here a bucket-list favourite. Come in winter for the most eye-popping white palette you'll ever see, but wrap up: temperatures average -5°C to -20°C (23°F to -4°F) through the day).

HOKKAIDO, Japan

The regal red-crowned crane is one of the rarest cranes in the world, and in Japan, it's cherished as a symbol of good luck and long life. While the breeding range centres on the border of China and Russia, a resident population is found in the marshlands of the Kushiro Shitsugen National Park, in eastern Hokkaido.

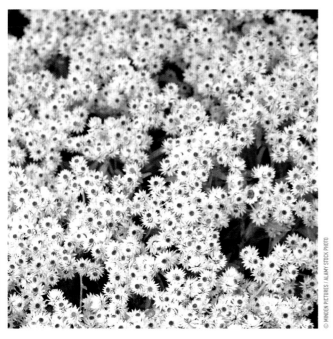

© RM FLORAL / ALAMY STOCK PHOTO

© MINDEN PICTURES / ALAMY STOCK PHOTO

LENÇÓIS MARANHENSES NP, Brazil

Brazil's north Atlantic coast is a long way from the sun-kissed beaches of Rio, but in the Lençóis Maranhenses National Park, it has a natural attraction not found anywhere else in this huge country; a vast desert landscape of rolling white sand dunes which contrasts strikingly with lagoons and mangrove swamps.

HOKKAIDO, Japan

Powder hunters love to experience the peaks around Niseko on Hokkaido, the northernmost of Japan's main islands. Up to 15m (600 inches) of snow falls a year here, and thanks to the moisture from the Sea of Japan hitting the cold winds from Siberia, the so-called *ja-pow* has the perfect dry, fluffy texture for skiing. Après-ski sessions in the area's many *onsen* are a welcome bonus.

CAMARGUE NATURAL PARK, France

The sight of the ancient breed of horse indigenous to the Camargue in southern France is something to behold, especially in the Camargue Natural Park, where horses, migrating birds such as pink flamingos and local people coexist in a natural paradise of wetlands, natural lakes and marshes.

MT EREBUS, Antarctica
A steaming ice fumarole above Sauna Cave at 3550m (11,647ft) on Mt Erebus, the southernmost active volcano on Earth. Heat from magma in the volcano melts the snow and ice beneath the ice towers to form striking caves and tunnels. Above ground, with air temperatures typically colder than –30°C (–22°F), the water vapour freezes into these distinctive towers of ice.

NORMANDY, France
The quintessential French biscuit, the macaron, is given the gourmet treatment at Michelin Bib Gourmand restaurant Manoir de la Pommeraie in Vivre, where gorgeous food is served up in an 18th-century stone house in a lovely rural setting, courtesy of a pastry chef who brings her Japanese heritage to this macaron with strawberry and yuzu.

DOHA, Qatar
Architect IM Pei brought the same skills used on the Louvre pyramid to Qatar's Museum of Islamic Art, which houses the largest collection of Islamic art in the world. Shaped like a postmodern fortress, it's an elegant, light-filled space that offers beauty both inside and out, with a grand palm-tree-lined entrance and views across the Corniche.

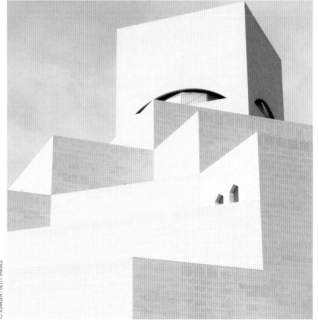

CHAMONIX, France

As the highest mountain in the Alps, 4808m (15,774ft) high Mont Blanc offers beautiful views for hikers year-round, but in winter, it's particularly unforgettable. Chamonix, as well as being renowned for its skiing, currently offers more than 200 hikes, including one on the snowy edge of the Aiguille du Midi, accessed by cable cars. Go with a guide.

UTAH, USA

The densely packed salt pan of the Bonneville Salt Flats is 1.5m (5ft) deep in places, and is the largest of the numerous salt flats west of Utah's Great Salt Lake basin. The figures are impressive, including an estimated 133 million tonnes (147 million tons) of salt, and land-speed records are chased every summer in a range of different events.

PISA, Italy

With its near-four-degree lean, Italy's Leaning Tower of Pisa looks preposterous as well as downright precarious, but it manages to be dignified too, perhaps because its accompanying cathedral and baptistry create such a unified whole. Still, you'll definitely need to take that photo where you're holding it up, before heading for Italy's other famous leaning attraction, the Due Torri of Bologna.

HOHENSCHWANGAU, Germany
Is it the original inspiration for the classic Disney film *Cinderella?* Or even for Sleeping Beauty's castle in Disneyland? Walt did visit Bavaria's 19th-century Romanesque-revival Neuschwanstein Castle before constructing his theme park, and there is an uncanny resemblance. We're not sure whether its maker, King Ludwig II of Bavaria, would have loved or loathed the appropriation.

WAITANGI, New Zealand
February 6th is a very special day in the North Island town of Waitangi. It's the date New Zealand commemorates the signing of the Treaty of Waitangi, regarded as the country's founding document. Here at the Waitangi Treaty Grounds the formal ceremony includes this naval salute, but elsewhere Kiwis let rip; in Auckland, 90,000 LEDs illuminate Harbour Bridge with stunning Maori imagery.

ARCTIC RUSSIA, Russia
Cute but tough, Russia's Arctic foxes survive some of the most frigid temperatures on the planet, only starting to shiver when the temperature drops to -70°C (-94°F), thanks to some serious padding (even their foot pads are covered in fur). Whether they'll be tough enough to survive the increasing red fox population in their breeding grounds — a result of climate change — remains to be seen.

WASHINGTON, DC, USA
There's the White House, then there's this white house: Washington's US Capitol Building. Arguably, as the home of the United States Congress and the seat of the legislative branch of the US federal government, it's the more important of the two. Today's dome, dating from 1855, is as impressive as it is iconic, standing three times the height of the original.

WASHINGTON, DC, USA
With a design inspired by a line from Martin Luther King Jr's *I Have A Dream* speech — 'Out of the mountain of despair, a stone of hope' — this memorial sculpture by Chinese artist Lei Yixin stands as a dignified and powerful tribute to the extraordinary civil rights leader. You'll find it in Washington's West Potomac Park near the United States National Mall.

PAMUKKALE, Turkey *(facing page)*
Denizli's 'cotton castle', aka the Pamukkale geothermal terraces, are regarded as the eighth wonder of the world by the Turkish. And they may have a point; the shimmering, snow-white limestone, shaped over millennia by calcium-rich springs forming milky blue hot pools, is surely one of the world's most beautiful sights. It's certainly one of its most photographed.

SIENA, Italy
Cypress trees stand guard along a white road cutting through rolling green pastures… it can only be Tuscany. The white road is a typical feature of the Crete Senesi, a clay-heavy area to the south of Siena characterised by distinctive white–grey soil across a range of hills and woods dotted with picture-postcard villages and the stunning monastery of Monte Oliveto Maggiore.

QUÉBEC, Canada

Canada's Arctic waters are the playground for all manner of marine life, among it the beluga whale, nicknamed the sea canary for its high-pitched whistles and clicks. For reliable sightings, head to the coastline of north and east Canada, such as Québec's Gulf of St Lawrence and Hudson Bay, where populations are stable and easily spotted from the coast.

CHIANG RAI, Thailand

Part traditional Buddhist temple, part wedding cake, Wat Rong Khun in Thailand's Chiang Rai is the surreal work of local artist Chalermchai Kositpipat, whose fanciful imagination led him to include a bridge over a field of fangs, hundreds of pleading arms and suffering faces of statues reaching up from hell. Gold rules the roost inside; even in the toilets.

TAIPEI, Taiwan

The serene outline of the Chiang Kai-shek Memorial Hall was erected in Taiwan's Taipei in memory of Chiang Kai-shek. The 'Generalissimo' was the leader of the Republic of China between 1928 and 1975, first in mainland China and then in Taiwan, until his death. The white stairs leading to the main entrance number 89, marking his age when he died here.

© JUSTIN FOULKES / LONELY PLANET

NEW MEXICO, USA
Located in New Mexico's Chihuahuan Desert, White Sands National Park is, at 712 sq km (275 sq miles), a vast landscape of blinding white gypsum dunes. Thanks to its previous status as a national monument, it's well maintained with lots of walking tracks and, if you're lucky, you might even see a launch from the missile-testing ranges found within it.

AGRA, India
The world's most romantic building? No contest. The ivory-white marble mausoleum that is the iconic Taj Mahal was completed in 1653 by the Mughal emperor Shah Jahan to house the body of his beloved wife, Mumtaz Mahal and, almost 400 years on, they lie here next to each other. Awww. Even the hordes of tourists can't detract from its serene beauty.

RIO DE JANEIRO, Brazil
It's arguably not as famous as the northern hemisphere's *David* by Michelangelo (see p170), but the southern hemisphere's most famous statue, *Cristo Redentor*, or Christ the Redeemer, has by far the better views, towering as it does over Rio de Janeiro from its perch on the peak of the 700m (2300ft) Corcovado mountain.

© GRAPHIXEL / GETTY IMAGES

© GAVIN HELLIER / AWL IMAGES LTD

© PHILIP LEE HARVEY / LONELY PLANET

© ANDREW MONTGOMERY / LONELY PLANET

© JUSTIN FOULKES / LONELY PLANET

LESBOS, Greece
A traditional Greek salad: a simple marriage of perfectly ripe vegetables and feta cheese, glistening with the best-quality extra virgin olive oil. Does it get any better than this? Yes, when it's being eaten in the Aegean — in this case at Sigri's harbourside Cavo Doro on the Greek island of Lesbos.

SANTORINI, Greece
In the pantheon of tumbling white towns set against sparkling blue seas, the Greek Cyclades island of Santorini is surely the most famous. The particularly cute collection of blue-doored sugar-cube houses of its two principal towns, Fira and Oia, always make for magical sunset shots.

MALLORCA, Spain
The Balearic island of Mallorca bursts into delicate white and pale pink bloom between January and February, with the flowering of hundreds of thousands of almond trees. It's Mallorca's version of snow, filling the landscape with colour and a sweet perfume, and adding an extra dimension to the already-spectacular hikes in the Serra de Tramuntana.

HLUBOKÁ CASTLE, Czech Republic
Modelled loosely on England's Windsor Castle, South Bohemia's Hluboká nad Vltavou Chateau belies its age, looking decidedly older than its youthful 150. It was commissioned by Johann Adolf II von Schwarzenberg, whose descendents lived here until the start of WWII, when then owner Adolph Schwarzenberg — an outspoken critic of Nazi Germany — left the country.

SEVILLE, Spain
During Easter week, or Semana Santa, Nazareno processions are a common sight throughout Spain, where mass mourning and public repentance of sins are put on display for all to see — albeit with faces hidden in shame behind these ghostly costumes. At the culmination of the week on Easter Sunday, tons of rose petals and sweets brighten up proceedings no end.

PUNTA TOMBO NATIONAL RESERVE, Argentina
Is there any natural sight more delightful than Emperor penguins at play in the depths of coastal Antarctica, where they withstand temperatures as low as −60°C (−76°F)? Too cold? Other species are much easier to spot in slightly warmer climes. On Argentina's eastern coast, Punta Tombo National Reserve is home to half a million Magellanic penguins from late September to April.

ALBEROBELLO, Italy

Unique to the Itria Valley in Puglia, *trulli* are some of the sweetest homes imaginable, their dry stone white limestone walls and comical conical roofs suggesting Hobbitish or other mythical inhabitants. In Alberobello, the collection of some 1500 of them, some dating as far back as the 14th century, has earned the town Unesco world heritage status.

SHANGHAI, China

Making the transition from northern Chinese villages to hipster food markets worldwide, fluffy white steamed *baozi*, or bao buns, are utterly moreish, whether moulded around traditional fillings like pork, red-bean paste, vegetables or potatoes, or more inventive 21st-century options like sweet squishy custard and, er, barbecued pigtails.

DOVER, England

Dover's White Cliffs are an iconic part of Britain's WWII history, and have been a beloved sight of Brits returning across the English Channel for decades, if not centuries. Walking at 107m (350ft) along the top of the chalk cliff face to the South Foreland Lighthouse affords spectacular views across the Channel, sometimes as far as France.

BERLIN, Germany
Located on the corner of Friedrichstraße and Zimmerstraße, Checkpoint Charlie once marked the best-known crossing point between Cold War East Berlin and West Berlin, being the only checkpoint through which diplomatic personnel, American military and non-German visitors could pass into East Berlin. The original hut is now located in the Allied Museum, but this replica still resonates.

SALAR DE UYUNI, Bolivia
Harsh, desolate and swept by cold winds, the surreal Salar de Uyuni, 3600m (11,800ft) high up in the Andes, is the world's largest salt-encrusted area. It's not all white though; the nearly 11,000 sq km (4247 sq miles) blinding white landscape is studded with red and green lagoons, giant cacti, hot springs and plenty of pink flamingos.

MIHINTALE, Sri Lanka
Proudly perched on a mountain peak near Anuradhapura, the sacred site of Mihintale, the cradle of Buddhism in Sri Lanka, houses a number of shrines and buildings, including the Ambasthala Dagoba stupa, and to its side, a flight of rock-carved steps leading to an appropriately large and serene looking statue of Buddha.

GREY

TROLLTUNGA, Norway

It's a strenuous 23–27km (14–16 mile) hike with an ascent of about 900m (2952ft) to the famous Trolltunga ('troll's tongue') rock in Skjeggedal, and while we can't recommend copying this man's insouciant stance at the tongue's tip (yes, people have fallen), it's worth the climb for breathtaking views over Lake Ringedalsvatnet.

COUNTY ANTRIM, Northern Ireland

The 40,000, 60-million-year-old hexagonal columns of the Giant's Causeway are, in a very real sense, monumental, their sculptural forms, breadth and scale seemingly so manufactured that you can't believe they're not the cosmic joke of some ancient extraterrestrial sculptor. Or maybe, just maybe, the work of the giant Finn MacCool that the causeway is named for.

FLATEY, Iceland

This ball of eider-duck feathers, harvested from birds in northwest Iceland's Breiðafjörður bay, is collected from the nests of wild common eiders. The process is highly regulated, with small groups of trained harvesters gently displacing the eggs in the nest and replacing the eider with a new nest lining before putting the eggs back in the nest.

KIZHI ISLAND, Russia *(previous page)*

The stunning 22 domes of the wooden Transfiguration Church, part of the 18th-century Kizhi Pogost complex, which includes a smaller nine-dome church and a bell-tower. Remarkably, all were constructed solely of interlocking wood, with nails used just in the domes and roof shingles. Find them in Lake Onega, some 480km (300 miles) northeast of St Petersburg.

BERLIN, Germany

The Denkmal für die Ermordeten Juden Europas (Memorial to the Murdered Jews of Europe). Arranged in a grid pattern across an uneven 19,000m² (4.7 acre) site, the 2,711 concrete slabs and columns, or 'stelae', create a disorienting effect that resembles nothing less than a medieval cemetery with sunken and collapsed headstones and graves uprooted to a bleak sci-fi setting.

VERDUN, France

The area around Verdun is filled with WWI sites, including this evocative battlefield trench. Other sombre memorials include an ossuary with an estimated 130,000 skeletons, the several kilometres of tunnels under Fort Douaumont, craggy machine gun turrets and bunkers and, in Verdun itself, the imposing Victory Monument, set into the town walls.

BESAKIH, Indonesia

One of the arresting pyramid-shaped Besakih temples, used as a Hindu place of worship from 1284, but thought to date back around two thousand years. It's just one of a *pura* (temple) complex made up of 23 temples, which taken together form the most important Hindu site in Bali. Perched 1000m (3280ft) up the slope of the active volcano Mount Agung, a visit here makes for a memorable outing.

GOÐAFOSS, Iceland

In a country famed for its waterfalls, which are the must-sees? Many would say the horseshoe basin of Goðafoss, in northern Iceland — not least for its legendary role in the country's history when, more than 1000 years ago, a leader helped bring Christianity to the island by throwing statues of the Norse gods into its roiling waters.

SVALBARD, Norway

This statue of Roald Amundsen in the remote village of Ny-Ålesund on Svalbard is a memorial to the Norwegian explorer and researcher who set out from here to reach the North Pole in 1925 and again in 1926, when he succeeded with the airship Norge. The village is still an important centre for Arctic research and environmental monitoring.

BOROBUDUR, Indonesia

The impressive central concrete stupa of Borobudur on Java, with the volcanic peak of Merapi in the background. Dating from the 9th century, the stupas are decorated with an impressive 2672 relief panels, and surrounded by 72 smaller openwork stupas, all constructed of interlocking masonry. Set majestically on a hilltop over lush green fields, it's an unforgettable sight.

© MATT MUNRO / LONELY PLANET

JÖKULSÁRLÓN, Iceland
Known as Diamond Beach for the sparkling ice crystals and floes that wash onto it from the Jökulsárlón Glacier Lagoon, Breiðamerkursandur (literally 'black-sand beach') is a must-do on Iceland's south coast. It's a spectacular non-stop five-hour drive from Rejykjavik, along the southern stretch of one of the world's greatest ring roads.

LONDON, England
The sleek, modernist Royal Festival Hall, opened in 1951 as part of the Festival of Britain and later joined by the more brutalist buildings that make up the Southbank Centre. Inside, the similarity to a cruise ship is a deliberate design element that referenced the rising popularity of the glamorous transatlantic crossings in post-war Britain.

JAVA, Indonesia
Painted wooden or leather *wayang* shadow puppets can be seen across Indonesia, and have been part of the culture for a millennium, according to evidence found in medieval texts and archeological sites. They're popular to this day, with their dramatic narratives accompanied by a gamelan orchestra and skillfully played out by a *dalang*, or puppeteer.

© EKO SETYAWAN / SHUTTERSTOCK

© LOOP IMAGES / GETTY IMAGES

HUA HIN, Thailand
Buddhist monk Luang Phor Thuad sits meditatively atop Wat Huay Mongkol near the beach resort of Hua Hin. A legendary southern Thai *bhikkhu* revered for his enlightenment and ability to perform miracles, including turning seawater into drinking water, the amulets bearing his image are popular with devotees who believe it will protect them in times of distress.

ABU DHABI, UAE
French architect Jean Nouvel's Louvre Abu Dhabi, opened on Saadiyat Island in November 2017, is striking for its gigantic, seemingly unsupported disc. Constructed in Nouvel's signature aluminium and stainless steel, it filters bright sunlight down in a way that, he says, was inspired by 'the way light filters through the roof of a souk or the leaves of a palm tree.'

DONNA NOOK NATIONAL NATURE RESERVE, England *(facing page)*
Grey seals abound on England's east coast, particularly at the Donna Nook National Nature Reserve in Lincolnshire, where from late October to December thousands of the semiaquatic mammals clamber on to the more than 10km (6.25 miles) of coastline between Grainthorpe Haven and Saltfleet sand dunes to give birth to their pups.

LOFOTEN ISLANDS, Norway
If you come to Lofoten in late spring or early summer, be prepared for a distinctly fishy smell in the air around you. For between February and May, the fish landed here are turned into stockfish – air-dried cod – by being dried outdoors on thousands of wooden racks for three months. After that, they're left to continue drying for up to a year indoors.

PATAGONIA NATIONAL PARK, Chile
This fire-eyed diucon in Valle Chacabuco, part of the Patagonia National Park, is named for its red iris. You'll find it perched on exposed branches in open woodland. The park was donated to the Chilean government in 2019 by the Tompkins Conservation Foundation as part of its program of protecting wildernesses.

GEGHARD, Armenia *(facing page)*
The striking *gavit* (entrance hall) of Armenia's Geghard cave monastery, built between 1215 and 1225, is just one part of a complex that illustrates Armenian medieval architecture at its highest point. The location, at the entrance to the soaring peaks and valleys of the Azat Valley, is stunning too.

LIÈGE, Belgium
Spanish architect Santiago Calatrava's vaulted glass and steel canopy over the Liège-Guillemins railway station is an arresting and elegant sight, but it's his innovative use of concrete, moulded and sculpted directly on site (a technique also used at London's Southbank Centre in the 1960s) to create the undulating structure, that gained him the most plaudits.

BRUSSELS, Belgium
The tiny Manneken Pis, making an increasingly rare naked appearance. Now a venerable 300 years old, Jérôme Duquesnoy's 61cm (24in) bronze cupid (actually a replica from 1965) is seen in suits as many as 130 days of the year. To see more than 1000 of the outfits, head for the GardeRobe MannekenPis costume museum. And to see the real *Putto* (small boy), visit the Brussels City Museum.

© PEKY / SHUTTERSTOCK

© RPBAIAO / SHUTTERSTOCK

© BRIAN MAUDSLEY / SHUTTERSTOCK

VESTURDALUR, Iceland

To properly understand the connection between Hallgrímskirkja church, Harpa Hall and Iceland's landscape, a visit to the valley of Vesturdalur, and in particular the basalt caves, pinnacles and rock formations at Hljóðaklettar, is a must. The Rauðhólar crater row, ponds of Eyjan and Jökulsárgljúfur canyon are added bonuses, and it all makes fantastic hiking territory.

HARPA, Iceland

The Harpa concert hall shimmers on the water's edge, its form both reflecting the sky and sea of coastal Reykjavík and referencing Iceland's basalt rock formations and monolithic landscapes. Artist Olafur Eliasson had a large hand in its 2011 creation. It's home to Icelandic Opera, the Iceland Symphony Orchestra, shops and restaurants.

HALLGRÍMSKIRKJA, Iceland

If Harpa looks to Iceland's future, Hallgrímskirkja church, designed by the late Guðjón Samúelsson in 1937, is very much about its past. Like Harpa, though, the church's form engages with Icelandic landscapes, with Samúelsson citing the shapes and forms of basalt, as well as Iceland's mountains and glaciers, as inspiration.

ALDABRA, Seychelles
There is something utterly magical about cycling around a car-free island only to be brought to a halt by an Aldabra giant tortoise lumbering across the road. Like the sound of it? Head for Aldabra or, more easily, one of the increasing number of Seychelles islands they live on, including North, Cousin and Curieuse islands, and La Digue.

YELLOWSTONE NATIONAL PARK, USA
Away from the well-worn tourist trails around Old Faithful, in Yellowstone's remote Lamar Valley in Wyoming, grey wolves are on the rise, making it the best place in the continental USA to see a wild wolf. For the best chance of seeing a member of the so-called Lamar Canyon wolf pack, visit in winter (December–February).

SAN DIEGO, USA
Named after Audrey and Theodor Seuss Geisel (aka children's author Dr Seuss), this hulking behemoth of reinforced concrete, the Geisel Library, is the main library building of the University of California San Diego. Its eight-storey brutalist tower was designed in the late 1960s by William Pereira to look like hands holding up a stack of books.

SÓLHEIMASANDUR, Iceland
Visiting here may seem a bit like dark tourism, but this plane wreck from a 1973 US Navy crash on the black Sólheimasandur beach in South Iceland happily resulted in no deaths. The monotone contrasts of the grey fuselage on jet-black or snowy white landscapes is decidedly film-like; albeit one of those grimly post-apocalyptic ones.

FLORENCE, Italy
Thousands of years after his creation, Michelangelo's David still manages to impress as he disdainfully averts his gaze from the teeming hordes 5m (17ft) below him in the Galleria dell'Accademia. Amazingly, he was carved from one block of marble, quarried from the Carrara quarries in Tuscany, which had previously been rejected by two other sculptors.

NKHOTAKOTA RESERVE, Malawi *(facing page)*
This gorgeous creature is part of a heartwarming tale that has seen the Nkhotakota Wildlife Reserve go from almost no elephants 15 years ago to some 500 today, thanks to a restocking programme from two other parks in 2015. Each elephant travelled 350km from Liwonde or 600km from Majete to get to its new home.

USHIKU, Japan
Fifty kilometres (31 miles) northeast of Tokyo, the beatific Ushiku Daibutsu stands 120m (394ft) tall, making it one of the five tallest statues in the world. Ride the elevator to the viewing gallery 85m (279ft) up, from where, on a clear day, you might spot the spindly spike of the Tokyo Skytree, or, if it's 15 August, enjoy the annual light show and fireworks display.

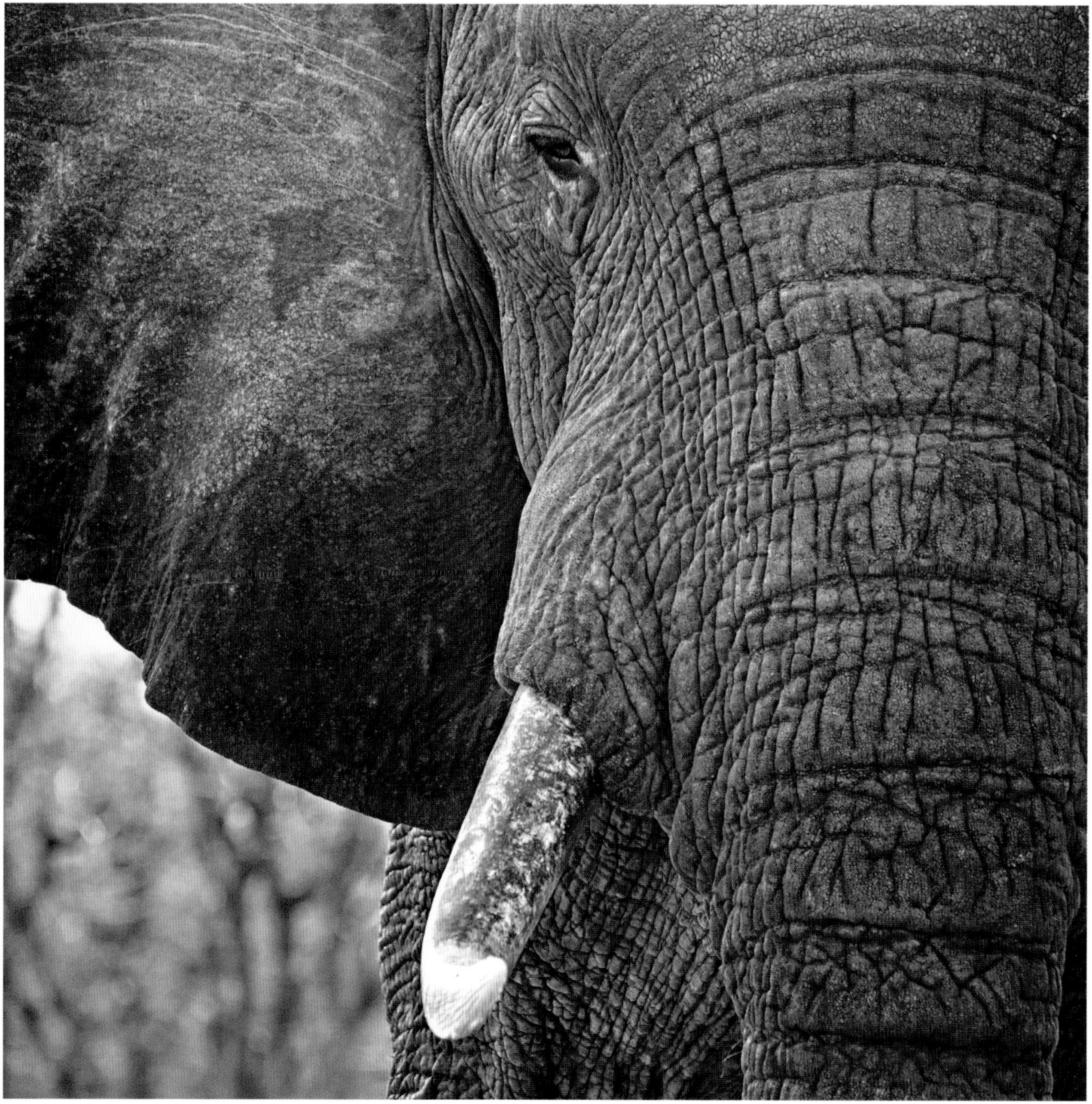

KANGAROO ISLAND, Australia

Kangaroo Island's abundant animal population — koalas included — has made it a booming wildlife-spotting destination, but tourism here was hit hard after half its land area was ravaged by devastating bushfires in 2019/2020. Taking the 45-minute ferry ride from the mainland is a great way help to boost the recovering economy and support efforts to care for the remaining 25,000 resident koalas.

STAVANGER, Norway

These 10m (33ft) bronze swords embedded in Stavanger rock, designed by local artist Fritz Roed, majestically mark the Battle of Hafrsfjord in 872 in an equally majestic setting. The battle united Norway as a single kingdom under the rule of one king, represented by the largest sword (the two smaller ones representing the losing kings).

MINSK, Belarus

Perhaps taking its cue from Minsk's astonishing collection of buildings that physically embodied Stalin's tenets of communism, the stolid rhombicuboctahedron form of the National Library of Belarus contains 22 floors, a book museum, and an observation point reached via an external glass lift. Bring a valid passport and you can even join the library.

STARA ZAGORA, Bulgaria
Symbolically lighting the way to the derelict UFO-shaped Buzludzha Monument high above it, this typically bombastic example of socialist realism marks the start of a treat for fans of brutalist concrete. From here, it's a few steep kilometres to the monument and the decaying remnants of its huge mural mosaics glorifying communist leaders.

PARIS, France
From the Galeries Lafayette rooftop or the top of the Centre Pompidou, the emblematic zinc rooftops of Paris's elegant 19th-century Haussmannian apartment buildings and grand 17th-century townhouses roll out in front of your eyes like a carpet of silver. No wonder they inspired Van Gogh and so many other artists.

LISBON, Portugal
Beautiful to look at, treacherous underfoot, Lisbon's hand-laid limestone mosaic cobblestones in Rossion Square and beyond have become one of the city's most famous symbols. But the *calçadas* have also been taken up enthusiastically across South America, most famously in Rio de Janeiro, on a 2.5km (1.5 mile) long stretch flanking Copacabana Beach.

© GERHARD ZWERGER-SCHONER / ROBERT HARDING

DALAT, Vietnam
The Hang Nga guesthouse, aka the Crazy House Hotel, is, as you might expect, as crazy inside as it is out. Themed sculpted rooms, connected by spindly bridges rising out of a tangle of greenery and lit by spiderweb windows, with swooping hand rails resembling jungle vines, can either be stayed in or visited on guided tours.

SVALBARD, Norway *(facing page)*
Northern fulmars glide above the breaking waves over a boat making its way from Pyramiden to the small coal-mining town of Longyearbyen in Norway's Svalbard archipelago. The birds nest in numerous cliffs around the coast and fjords of Svalbard — visit in February for the best chance of seeing them there.

SOUTH DAKOTA, USA
The sight of George Washington, Thomas Jefferson, Abraham Lincoln and Theodore Roosevelt iconically staring out from the hugely popular Mount Rushmore National Memorial never fails to impress, particularly when you take in the sheer scale of the granite enterprise, created by American sculptor Gutzon Borglum and a team of labourers between 1927 and 1941.

TRAZBON, Turkey
The Sümela Monastery, set 1200m (4000ft) above sea level in the Pontic Mountains, was partially reopened in 2019 after comprehensive restoration work. With an eye to the popularity of the area with walkers, part of that work has included the restoration of a hiking path enabling better access to this majestic medieval Greek Orthodox monastery.

© HAEREE PARK / SHUTTERSTOCK

© AYHAN ALTUN / ALAMY STOCK PHOTO

KYOTO, Japan

One of the Daitoku-ji temple complex's many zen rock gardens. Only four of its temples — Ryogen-in, Zuiho-in, Daisen-in and Koto-in — are open year round, but their gardens are enough to satisfy the keenest spiritual horticulturalists. Ryogen-in contains the best range, but don't miss Zuiho-in's famous dry landscape gardens and Koto-in, renowned for its entryway.

DETTIFOSS, Iceland

The roaring power of the Dettifoss waterfall in the Vatnajökull National Park, where meltwater from the biggest ice cap in Europe creates a spectacular landscape. Bring an anorak and sturdy boots, and prepare to get wet. If the majestic setting looks familiar as you gaze down from the viewing platform, it may be from Ridley Scott's *Prometheus* — the falls feature in the opening scene.

BAJA CALIFORNIA, Mexico *(facing page)*

An adult grey whale breaches the blue waters off Baja California. Each year whales travel more than 16,000km (10,000 miles) to get here, coming to give birth and raise their young in sheltered coastal lagoons. Catch them from January to March, and add some context to your trip with a visit to the Museo de la Ballena (the Whale Museum) in La Paz.

ANTANANARIVO, Madagascar

A ring-tailed lemur, endemic to Madagascar, sits on a tree stump. The species includes the smallest primate in the world, Madame Berthe's mouse lemur, which averages a tiny 9cm (3.6in) in body length. It, and most of Madagascar's lemurs, are threatened with extinction, but conservationists believe responsible ecotourism might save them. So what are you waiting for?

© DENNISVDW / GETTY IMAGES

© PAVEL ILYUKHIN / SHUTTERSTOCK

© IGNACIO PALACIOS / GETTY IMAGES

TSINGY DE BEMARAHA NATIONAL PARK, Madagascar

A tourist crosses a rope bridge spanning the unique limestone karsts of the Tsingy de Bemaraha National Park, in northwest Madagascar's Melaky Region. The needle-shaped limestone pinnacles, appropriately named 'Tsingy' — or 'the place where one cannot walk barefoot' — can be visited during the dry season from April to November.

EASTER ISLAND, Chile

Easter Island's monolithic *moai* have been standing guard over their eastern Polynesia territory for up to 900 years. Most of the island now forms the Rapa Nui National Park, where 887 volcanic rock heads and figures generate revenue which, for the first time in history, is now invested in the island and used to conserve its natural heritage.

ROME, Italy

The domed roof of Rome's perfectly proportioned Pantheon, with its famous open aperture, or oculus, in the top. The 7.8m (25ft) diameter hole is, remarkably, the only light source in the building. Undoubtedly the best-preserved ancient Roman monument in the city, the dome remains the largest unsupported one in the world at 43.3m (142ft).

© DREAMSTATION / GETTY IMAGES

MYSORE, India
Mysore's Sri Nandi Temple in southern India venerates Nandi, the bull companion/mount of Lord Shiva, with this impressive granite fellow set atop a hill with great views over the lush vegetation of Karnataka. Believed to be as much as 350 years old and carved from a single block of granite, he rises up more than 4m (15ft), with a girth of more than 7m (24ft).

GALÁPAGOS ISLANDS, Ecuador
Charles Darwin described the marine iguanas he met on his travels as 'imps of darkness'. Today we have more regard for these unique lizards, which sunbathe on the rocky shore before plunging into the cool ocean to graze on algae on the sea bed. Belly-full but body-cold, they clamber back up for another dose of warming sunshine.

SARDINIA, Italy
Forget Venice: the ancient Mamuthones festival of Mamoiada takes masked revelry somewhere much deeper. The sombre ritual, which takes place three time a year around Lent, involves men dressing in black sheepskin and loading themselves with 30kg (66lbs) of cowbells before donning a dark wooden mask to parade the streets, in a ritual believed to be 2000 years old.

© PHILIP LEE HARVEY / LONELY PLANET

© AGB PHOTO LIBRARY / ALAMY STOCK PHOTO

INDEX

ACKNOWLEDGMENTS

TRAVEL BY COLOUR

September 2020

Published by Lonely Planet Global Limited

CRN 554153

www.lonelyplanet.com

10 9 8 7 6 5 4 3 2 1

Printed in Singapore

ISBN 978 1788 68917 5

© Lonely Planet 2020

© photographers as indicated 2020

Managing Director, Publishing Piers Pickard

Associate Publisher Robin Barton

Art Director Daniel Di Paolo

Writer Yolanda Zappaterra

Image Researcher Regina Wolek

Editor James Smart

Cover images: © Matthew Williams-Ellis, © Wibowo Rusli / Alamy Stock Photo, © Peetatham Kongkapech / Getty Images , © moorhen / Getty Images, © tunart / Getty Images, © Imagevixen / Getty Images, Mark Read / Lonely Planet, Philip Lee Harvey / Lonely Planet, Mark Read / Lonely Planet, © Pipat Kamma / Shutterstock, © Matthias Kestel / Shutterstock, © Hagen Production / Shutterstock, © Krzyza / Shutterstock

LONELY PLANET OFFICES

AUSTRALIA
The Malt Store, Level 3,
551 Swanston St, Carlton, Victoria 3053
T: 03 8379 8000

USA
Suite 208, 155 Filbert Street,
Oakland, CA 94607
T: 510 250 6400

IRELAND
Digital Depot, Roe Lane (off Thomas St),
Digital Hub, Dublin 8,
D08 TCV4

EUROPE
240 Blackfriars Rd,
London SE1 8NW
T: 020 3771 5100

STAY IN TOUCH lonelyplanet.com/contact

Paper in this book is certified against the Forest Stewardship Council™ standards. FSC™ promotes environmentally responsible, socially beneficial and economically viable management of the world's forests.